DISCOVERING
sauerkraut

Alice Walczyule

DISCOVERING
sauerkraut

ALICE WOLCZUK

The Caitlin Press

The Caitlin Press P.O. Box 2387, Station B Prince George, B.C.
V2N 2S6 Canada

Caitlin Press would like to acknowledge the financial support of the
Canada Council and the British Columbia Cultural Fund.

Canadian Cataloguing in Publication Data

Wolczuk, Alice, 1920- Discovering Sauerkraut

Includes bibliographical references and index. ISBN 0-920576-43-5

1. Cookery (Sauerkraut) I. Title. TX814.5.S37W64 1993   641.6'534
C93-091089-3

Cover, Interior Design and Illustrations by Gaye Hammond
Indexed by Kathy Plett
Typeset by Vancouver Desktop Publishing

Printed in Canada

This book is dedicated to my parents Alex and Margaret Hubensky who always believed I could do anything I wanted and to my friends at Willows Farm who encouraged and inspired me.

Contents

Introduction

"What is the main ingredient in sauerkraut?" was the question which turned up in game of Trivial Pursuit. So far, ten-year-old Jimmy had not had much success with his replies but the answer to this one he knew without a doubt. He wriggled in his chair, his face flushed with imminent success.

"Germans!" he yelled triumphantly.

Jimmy was on the right track but he hadn't made the right connection; neither did he come up with the right ingredient. The German language gave this universally accepted name for sour or salt-preserved cabbage, but there is no history of Germans having invented it.

The origins of salt preserving are lost in antiquity but the process has been used since the earliest of times, traces having been found dating back to hunter-gatherer days. Salt may be used to preserve fish, meats, and dairy products. No doubt, like so many other things, the process was discovered by accident. Salting, lactic acid fermentation, permitted the inhabitants of very hot countries to preserve foods in summer for use in winter, or lean times, centuries before refrigeration, canning, and freezing. We still enjoy foods prepared in this manner and continue with the practice.

There are many stories about the invention of sauerkraut. It is said that when the Great Wall of China was being built six thousand years ago, the peasants were promised their food and drink. Most of them were too poor to own more than one vessel so the food and drink —cabbage and some wine — invariably were dumped into one container. Some people noticed the change in flavor after a few days and decided it was pretty good.

If knowledge about the fermentation of cabbage began in China, it took a long time to travel across Asia to Europe. The Tartars, who supposedly learned about the process in China, developed their own method of making and using it. In their turn, the Tartars taught the process to peoples in central Europe, in the region of present-day

Austria and from there the knowledge and practice spread throughout Europe. Certainly the Slavic nations had it; and Pliny the Elder was said to have written about it around 50 A.D. Whatever way the knowledge of pickled cabbage travelled, the dish made a great difference to the people who used it, among them seafarers, for whom scurvy, caused by the lack of dietary vitamin C, was endemic and fatal on long voyages. Credit for the introduction of sauerkraut, along with citrus fruits and other foods high in vitamin C, on long voyages of exploration is attributed to Captain James Cook. Cook, a most humane ship's captain, lost only one man to scurvy in the one thousand days at sea during three voyages at the end of the eighteenth century.

Today we use lactic fermentation for a great many foods, including sour milk, buttermilk, and yogurt. The process is used the world over, including Africa, where the Masai ferment milk by putting it into gourds with some blood from cattle, a method which preserves the milk in the heat. Other nomadic groups use the same method; many other peoples use salting and fermentation not only for preserving their food, but to create the flavors they enjoy.

Lactic fermentation creates tasty, easily digested products. Not only are they good health foods, but they are also usually low in calories. Canned sauerkraut shows only the barest trace of fat, has a bit of protein, and is very low in carbohydrates, with only six grams per cup. In total, a cupful will count only thirty calories, an excellent choice, if you want to diet.

Certainly the European settlers who came to the North American prairies depended on sauerkraut as a much-needed vegetable during the winter months. Barrels of sauerkraut and dill pickles, the products of industriously tended summer vegetable gardens, were ubiquitous in prairie farm pantries, for neither cabbages or cucumbers kept well in dugouts under kitchen or living room floors, or even in root cellars.

The making of such a large amount of sauerkraut was a family affair. Often relatives or neighbors got together to help each other, happy to make the work a social occasion; settlers in the early days had few opportunities to meet socially as they were too busy making a living. I remember how exciting these occasions were. My father sharpened all the knives. A space was cleared for the cabbage. The cabbage cutter blade was removed, sharpened, and replaced, carefully adjusting it to make the right kind of cut. Mother scrubbed out the barrel, the rocks for pressing the cabbage in the barrel, and the pounder, while my sister and I got underfoot with great success. We were not allowed to cut the cabbage, although occasionally Father allowed us to try using the pounder, which we could barely lift. But we did get to taste the salted cabbage when Mother tasted it. She seemed to know when it was just right, and of course we couldn't be left out of the secret.

I cannot claim any great expertise as a cook, but I do love food and I am a zealous recipe collector for anything that sounds good. I try a good many of the recipes because I enjoy cooking although I am lazy and try to cook large meals so I don't have to cook every day.

The recipes in this book have been garnered from a great many sources over a long period of time. I have searched through books and magazines, spoken to strangers, friends, and relatives. The longer I collected recipes, the more surprised I was by the many ways of cooking sauerkraut. Even after I deemed my collection complete, I kept finding new variations. There are many areas I have not had the opportunity to research, including Oriental cuisine, which still uses salted cabbage, not as we do, but as a spice or condiment.

My search began for no other reason than to collect a few recipes for some friends at Willows Farm who were new at both making and using sauerkraut. To them, I am grateful for their suggestion that I continue to expand my collection.

Sauerkraut is one food that can be blended with almost any other ingredient; the only criterion is that the result must please the palate. Do not hesitate to experiment. If you don't like what you have created, you need not use the same combination of ingredients again. By substituting other ingredients on another occasion you may find that you have created a new, wonderfully tasty, prize-winning recipe.

I hope you enjoy experimenting with sauerkraut and eating the products of your ingenuity

Alice Wolczuk
Prince George, British Columbia
1994

Making Sauerkraut at Home

Making Sauerkraut at Home

There are several ways of making sauerkraut. In my childhood (it is still true today), each household had a favorite method and seasonings. Some would not consider adding anything but salt; others thought that salt was insufficiently tasty, and they would make many additions, such as pickling spice, peppercorns, apples, to name only a few.

Stone crocks and wooden barrels were the containers traditionally used to make and store sauerkraut. In the days before refrigeration, the barrels were put outdoors to keep the sauerkraut frozen during the winter months. This was necessary because although active fermentation had ceased, freezing counteracted the slow fermentation that continued indefinitely. When you needed some sauerkraut, you went outside, uncovered the barrel, and chopped out the amount required with a stout knife. Now we have easier ways of keeping it over winter.

Stone crocks are still excellent containers for making sauerkraut. If you are buying one second hand, examine the inside carefully for cracks and other blemishes. If it has a permanent whitish stain, it has been used to store eggs in waterglass, and this makes the container unsuitable for making sauerkraut as the waterglass residue inhibits fermentation.

There are recipes for making sauerkraut in jars or other large containers. You can purchase specially made "fermentation pots" which can relieve you of some of the work involved in keeping the air out of the fermenting cabbage.

Sauerkraut can be made in as large or as small quantities at a time as you wish. At home, we make large quantities so we always have some on hand.

All cabbages will make sauerkraut, but each has slightly different properties. Cabbages are roughly divided into types according to the number of growing days from transplantation to maturity. Early cabbages take from 56 to 70 days: mid-season from 70 to 76 days; and late cabbages from 76 to 99 days. Red cabbage is not generally used to make sauerkraut, neither are the savoy types.

Choose firm heads of cabbage. We usually chose firm, unblemished heads, but split heads, or those too deformed for sale or storage may also be used as long as they are firm and can be trimmed clean.

Do not wash the heads, but trim off the outer leaves until the head is clean.

Early Cabbage: Early cabbage is the most tender, and the heads are the best to cure for use in making cabbage rolls (holubtsi). This cabbage also makes the most tender sauerkraut, but one that does not keep long in storage.

Unfortunately, early cabbage matures so early that you may not be able to make use of it. Other disadvantages are that the heads split very quickly in the garden, often beyond redemption, and they do not keep well in storage.

Mid-Season Cabbage: This is still a tender cabbage. It matures later than the early cabbage, but is a couple of weeks earlier than the late. It does not split readily in the garden and it will store for a fairly long time. It makes good sauerkraut.

Late Cabbage: The heads of late cabbage keep well in storage for most of the winter, but they make the least tender sauerkraut, and they require more cooking. In spite of this, late cabbage is often made into sauerkraut because it is ready about the time that the garden work is slowing down.

It is the least desirable method for curing whole heads, but it does tenderize them somewhat.

Selecting the Cabbage

If you are growing your own cabbages, look for seed of some of the new introductions specially recommended for sauerkraut.

Some Essential Equipment

1. Some sturdy, sharp knives for splitting the cabbage.

2. A shredder is a boon if you are making a larger quantity of sauerkraut. Although shredders are not easily available these days, they might be found in country hardware stores, especially around harvest time. If you are making a small quantity, any utensil that will help you shred the cabbage quickly and easily would be useful.

3. A stamper or pounder is essential. It is most important to pound or mash the cabbage as this will make the difference between success or failure. When my parents got married and were ready to make their own sauerkraut, my father carved from oak a staff about 36 inches long and 4 inches in diameter, which allowed him to pound a barrel full of cabbage. It is still in use today. A stout wooden mallet would serve the same purpose. If you are making your sauerkraut in jars, use a potato masher.

4. Make sure that the containers, the utensils, and your hands are as clean as you can make them. Cleanliness is essential for successful fermentation.

5. A clean cloth big enough to fit over the shredded cabbage and the container.

6. A plate or board that will fit snugly inside the container.

7. A heavy weight to place on top of the plate or board. This makes sure that the brine rises above the plate. We always used a large stone which was scrubbed clean and used year after year.

Preparing the Cabbage

1. Choose mature, firm heads of cabbage. Remember that the highest concentration of vitamin C is in the green leaves.

2. Remove only the soiled outer leaves, and do not wash the cabbage as the wild yeast on the unwashed leaves helps with fermentation.

3. Set aside some of the clean outer leaves to top the shredded cabbage in your crock, then cut the heads in quarters and remove the cores. If you want to use the cores, shred them separately, then add to the cabbage. They impart a slightly different flavor. We never used them in the sauerkraut but it was a special treat to have them trimmed to eat raw.

4. Shred the cabbage on a shredder or with a strong, sharp knife or other utensil. Lately, I have discovered that my meat cleaver works beautifully. The shredded cabbage should be as fine as coleslaw or the thickness of a dime.

These preparations are basic to the process of fermenting cabbage, but there are several ways of making sauerkraut and some recipes follow.

The Wolczuk Family's Favorite Sauerkraut

While sauerkraut can be made without salt (see index), most sauerkrauts contain between .08% to 2% salt. My mother never measured the amount of salt she used in making sauerkraut, but judged by tasting the saltiness of the cabbage. The cabbage should be quite salty, but pleasantly so. Sometimes Mother's sauerkraut turned out a bit too salty but most of the time she was right on. For those with less confidence in their tastebuds than my mother had, here are some handy measurements stated by volume and metric, although the recipes in this collection use only standard volume measurements. Remember to use ONLY pickling salt or sea salt.

2 tsp salt to 1 lb cabbage or
10 mL salt to 500 g cabbage

1 lb salt to 40 lbs cabbage or
500 mL salt to 20 kg cabbage

1 1/2 cups salt to 40 lbs cabbage
3 Tbsp salt to 5 quarts cabbage or
45 mL salt to 5 L cabbage

Here's the way we made sauerkraut in my parent's home when I was a child.

Pack from 2-4 inches of shredded cabbage in your container, sprinkle the cabbage with salt, and mix the cabbage and salt thoroughly. Pound the cabbage/salt mixture with a mallet until you hear squishy sounds. Add more cabbage, and repeat the salting, mixing, and pounding until you have the desired amount of cabbage in the container. You will find that all your pounding efforts will have created a briny liquid which has come to the surface of the cabbage.

Cover the shredded cabbage with some of the whole cabbage leaves, and spread a clean cloth over the top of the leaves.

Place the plate or board over the cloth to keep air from the mixture, and weight the cover with a heavy stone. You should see the brine creep over the cloth onto the plate or board.

The stone crock or container should be placed in a warm spot—temperature between 68° F and 72° F (20° C and 21° C) is about right for good fermentation—and left there for between 2 to 6 weeks. At lower temperatures the cabbage will take longer to ferment; at higher temperatures, the process will be faster, but the finished sauerkraut will be of inferior quality.

During fermentation, a scum will form on the surface, the cloth, and the board, and this scum should be removed daily. Skim the scum off the surface, and wash the cloth and board in hot water before replacing them.

When bubbles stop rising to the surface of the cabbage and brine mixture, active fermentation has stopped. However, slow fermentation will continue, and the sauerkraut will become much stronger in flavor over a period of time. To stop this action, the sauerkraut must be frozen or canned in glass jars, following the manufacturer's directions.

Variations: Not everybody makes their sauerkraut plain without additions, although this is my favorite way. Many other vegetables may be included or prepared separately, and very tasty they are too. Just think of dill pickles!

Each country has its own favorite additions; for instance, the French like to include juniper berries. Some like to mix in a quantity of pickling spice; others like the tang of peppercorns. Any single whole spice can be added to your liking, or you can mix them in any combination.

If you are in the mood to experiment, add a few pieces of ginger root and lemons.

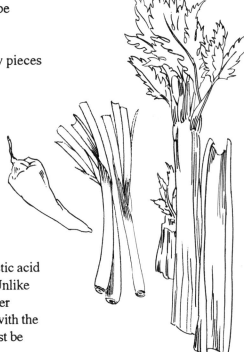

Here is a partial list of what you can add:
   pumpkin
   any of the root vegetables
   red, green, and chili peppers
   celery
   carrots
   onions
   horseradish
   radish

Most garden vegetables may be preserved by lactic acid fermentation, either separately or in combination. Unlike the cabbage which can be preserved saltless, all other vegetables must be salted. Use all vegetables raw, with the exception of green or yellow wax beans, which must be cooked for at least 5 minutes before being pickled.

Dill is a favorite herb to use, although others may be used also. Whole apples, unpeeled, are often included in a batch of sauerkraut. They are excellent to serve with pork.

Preferred Ingredients

In the days before button mushrooms were so readily available, many European people dried mushrooms for winter use. Dried mushrooms are still available today; they are stronger flavored than the fresh ones and must be used sparingly. The measurements I have given are for the whole pieces of mushrooms before they are soaked.

I like to use herb bouquets in cooking, and have included a section on herb bouquets (see index).

Hamburg parsley with the root is preferrable if it is available as it gives a better taste.

Holubtsi: If you desire whole cabbage heads for cabbage rolls (holubtsi), select small, firm heads, trim off the outer leaves, and remove the cores. The heads are then arranged in the crock in alternating layers with the shredded and pounded cabbage.

Sauerkraut from Chinese Cabbage

This method of sauerkraut comes from Illinois. It is similar to making sauerkraut in a jar and can be done in the same way.

Wash and sterilize several wide-mouth, one-quart canning jars, following the manufacturer's directions.

Shred the Chinese Cabbage with a very sharp knife. If you are making a large quantity, you may use a shredder on the solid part but the softer leaves will have to be finely sliced with a knife.

Pack the sterilized jars tightly, using a potato masher to pound down the cabbage. Fill to within an inch of the top and add 1 teaspoon of salt. Slowly fill the jars with boiling water, allowing the contents to settle. Insert a knife blade at intervals around the jar top to allow trapped air to escape. Leave one-half inch of space at the top of each jar.

Seal the jars tightly. During the fermentation process, set the jars in a plastic or enamelled dish to catch any excess juices which spill over the seal. Check daily and wipe off the jars, tightening the lids a little afterwards. Never loosen the lids, and avoid breaking the seals of the lids on jars where there is no evidence of a fresh leak. Fermentation is odorous, but there will be no odor when the sauerkraut is ready.

The Chinese cabbage should be checked in about 4 days to see if active fermentation has ceased. When the sauerkraut is cured, wash the jars, and store them in a cool, dark place.

For 5 quarts of Sauerkraut

Follow the same procedure used in Sauerkraut from Chinese Cabbage, noting that the fermentation process will take up to 6 weeks.

10 lbs dense, firm cabbage

$^1/_2$ cup pickling salt

Saltless Sauerkraut

This recipe is perfect for people who are unable to use much salt.

Shred the cabbage and pack it into a small crock. Fill the crock with cold water, covering the cabbage completely, but not more than 2 or 3 inches from the top.

Place a plate, or board cut to the proper size, to fit just inside the crock, pressing down over the cabbage until it is submerged. Weight it with some clean, sizeable stones. Cover the container with the clean cloth and set in a basin to catch the overflow.

It is important to start the fermentation process at a temperature of 68° F to 70° F (20° C to 21° C) for the first week, after which it may be put into a cooler place, about 60° F (16° C). Skim off any scum that may develop on the surface. Check the sauerkraut after 5 to 6 days, at which time it should be ready. If you like a stronger tasting product, let the cabbage ferment a little longer.

Variations:
- For each head of cabbage, add
  $^1/_2$ tsp each dill, celery, and caraway seeds
  1 tsp ground kelp.
  More flavor is added if you grind the seeds. You can use all of these, some, or none at all. Mix in well with the cabbage.

- To 15 lbs of cabbage add
  3 Tbsp lemon juice
  3 oz glucose

Storing Sauerkraut

In the past, before refrigeration and when canning jars were less plentiful, the containers of sauerkraut were put outdoors to freeze. It was fine until spring, but the sauerkraut soured rapidly once the warm weather arrived. Today, we stop the fermentation process by storing the sauerkraut in one of the following ways:

Freezing: Sauerkraut freezes well (over a year without freezer burn) and this is my favorite way of storing it.

Drain and pack the sauerkraut into suitably sized containers or bags. Fermentation does not stop entirely, and you will find that it tastes stronger in the spring than it did in the fall. One way to avoid some of this strong taste is to pack the sauerkraut before it reaches its full flavor.

Canning: Pack the sauerkraut into clean, sterilized jars and cover it with its own brine, leaving one-half inch space at each jar top. Seal the jars tightly with sterilized lids and check for leakage. This is very important.

If there is not enough brine to fill all the jars, make a solution of salt and water using 2 Tbsp coarse salt per quart of water. Stir until dissolved and top the sauerkraut with it to within one-half inch of the jar top.

Process the jars in a boiling water bath for 10 to 15 minutes, or in a pressure cooker for 5 minutes at 10 lbs pressure.

The Reasons for that Bad Batch

Too Soft

- too high a temperature while fermenting

- shredded too finely

- uneven distribution of salt

- poor fermentation due to airpockets caused by packing the cabbage improperly

Pink Fungus

- too much salt

- uneven distribution of salt

- improperly covered

- not weighted enough during fermentation

Rotten Or Dark Sauerkraut

- not properly packed

- not covered well enough to exclude air during fermentation

- insufficient brine to cover the fermenting cabbage

- too long a storage period
- too high a temperature during fermentation, processing, or storage.

Beverages and Appetizers

Beverages and Appetizers

Homemade sauerkraut contains no vinegar and provides the tastiest juice. Sauerkraut juice has been used as a thirst quencher in some European countries for many years. It is tart and pleasantly salty, excellent on a hot day, and is satisfying without any additions. A few herbs or a dash of Worcestershire sauce, however, will turn the sauerkraut juice into a tasty new drink.

Sauerkraut Tomato Cocktail

5-6 servings

2 cups sauerkraut juice

2 cups tomato juice

1/4 tsp chopped dill or parsley

pepper to taste

Put all the ingredients in a blender. Mix well. Chill before serving.

Variations:
- for extra nutrition, add 2-3 Tbsp nutritional yeast
- add a dash of Worcestershire Sauce to taste
- use V8 vegetable juice in place of plain tomato juice

Sauerkraut Juice Appetizer

3-4 servings

3 cups sauerkraut juice

3/4 cup unpeeled, diced apple

1/2 tsp caraway seeds (optional)

Here is another way to mix apple and sauerkraut. A bit of lemon juice enlivens this.

Blend all ingredients in a blender. Serve cold, garnished with a sprig of parsley.

Sauerkraut Pineapple Cooler

serves 5-6

For the hottest days, try this reviving blend of sweet and sour juices.

Blend all ingredients well. Chill before serving.

2 cups sauerkraut juice

2 cups pineapple juice

2 Tbsp lemon juice

1-2 tsp brown sugar, to taste

Sauerkraut Morsels

100 pieces

Hors d'oeuvres and canapes are served as appetizers. Part of the fun is to discover or invent new ways of making them. Preparing and serving seems to be as limitless as your imagination. Try these tasty tidbits and see if your guests can guess how you made them. Chop sauerkraut very finely and mix with the meats, onions, parsley, mustard, salt and pepper, and sugar. Cook this mixture in a large skillet over moderate heat until the meat is browned. Remove skillet from heat and stir in the bread crumbs. Slightly beat 1 egg and add to the meat mixture. Mix well and set aside to cool.

When cool, form into balls about the size of a walnut. Beat the remaining eggs together with the milk. Dip the balls into the egg mixture, then roll them in the crumbs, and place on a cookie sheet. Broil for about 1 minute then turn and broil on the other side.

The mixture can be prepared to the formation of the crumbed balls, refrigerated and broiled when needed.

2 $^1/_2$ to 3 cups sauerkraut

1 lb bulk pork sausage

$^1/_2$ lb lean ground beef

$^1/_2$ onion, finely chopped

3 Tbsp dried parsley

$^1/_2$ tsp dried mustard

$^1/_8$ tsp salt

$^1/_8$ tsp pepper

1 tsp sugar

$^3/_4$ cup dried bread crumbs

3 eggs

$^1/_4$ cup milk

bread crumbs for coating

Sauerkraut Balls

1 lb lean ground pork

1 lb ham

³/₄ lb corned beef

1 medium onion, quartered

3 Tbsp chopped fresh parsley

2 cups milk

1 ¹/₂ tsp dry mustard

1 tsp salt if needed

¹/₄ tsp monosodium glutamate (optional)

2 cups all-purpose flour

4-5 cups partially drained sauerkraut

2 eggs

2 Tbsp water

flour for coating

bread crumbs

oil for deep frying

Preparing these sauerkraut balls takes time, but they are well worth it. They can be made ahead of time as they freeze successfully. Thaw them quickly in the microwave. Great for parties, they can be served hot or cold.

Grind the meats, onion, and parsley. Fry the mixture in a skillet, stirring occasionally, until brown.

Add milk, dry mustard, salt, monosodium glutamate, and flour. Cook and stir until fluffy. Cool.

Add sauerkraut. Put the entire mixture through the food grinder once again; this ensures a fine texture in the finished product. Mix thoroughly.

Roll into balls about the size of a walnut. Beat eggs with 1 or 2 Tbsp water. Roll each ball in flour then dip into the egg and roll in fine bread crumbs. Deep fry in oil at 375° F until golden brown on all sides. Drain on paper towels. Serve warm.

Ham and Sauerkraut Croquettes

30-40 croquettes

This recipe can be doubled; the croquettes freeze well, and they can be reheated as required.

In a large skillet, fry the onion in butter over moderate heat until soft. Add the sauerkraut and cook for 3 minutes, stirring. Add the ham, caraway, dry mustard; season with salt and pepper to taste. Stir in the Béchamel sauce and blend well.

Beat in the egg yolks and cook until the mixture just reaches the boil. Spread on a buttered platter, cover with plastic wrap and chill. Shape into cone-shaped small croquettes.

Beat the water and egg in a bowl. Season with salt and pepper. Roll the croquettes in flour, then in egg mixture, then in crumbs. Let coating set.

Heat oil to 375° F and fry until golden. Drain on paper towels. Serve with the lemon wedges and hot mustard.

1/3 cup minced onion

1 Tbsp butter

2 cups sauerkraut, squeezed dry

2 cups finely ground cooked ham

1/2 tsp caraway seeds (optional)

2 1/2 tsp dry mustard

salt and pepper to taste

1/2 cup Béchamel sauce (recipe follows)

2 egg yolks

1/4 cup water

1 egg

all-purpose flour

1 1/2 cups dry bread crumbs

oil for deep frying

lemon wedges

hot mustard

Béchamel Sauce

Put the flour into a cup or a small bowl. Add a bit of the milk to the flour and beat to make a smooth paste. Put the milk and butter into a double boiler, and when it is brought to a boil, add the paste slowly, stirring briskly to prevent it from lumping. Season with salt and paprika to taste. Strain if necessary, before using.

1 1/2 Tbsp butter

2 Tbsp flour

1/2 cup milk

18 turnovers

Krautovers

2 Tbsp minced onion

1 Tbsp butter 1 cup drained sauerkraut

¹/₂ to ³/₄ cup ground cooked beef or ham

1 tsp minced dill pickle

Butter Pastry (recipe follows)

¹/₄ tsp marjoram

¹/₂ tsp ground thyme

¹/₂ tsp minced dill

salt and pepper to taste

1 egg

1 tsp sour cream

Fry the onion in butter until golden. Add the sauerkraut, meat, pickle, marjoram, thyme, dill, salt and pepper. When thoroughly hot, mix in the egg and sour cream, stirring constantly. Remove from heat and cool.

Roll out the pastry thinly; cut into rounds, 2 ¹/₂ inches in diameter or larger. Wet the edges with water, place a spoonfull of filling in the middle, then fold over to cover. Press the edges well together. Place on a cookie sheet. Bake in a medium oven, about 350 F until golden in color.

You can deep fry them if you wish.

2 cups sifted flour

1 tsp salt

¹/₄ lb butter

6 Tbsp cold water, chilled in the refrigerator

Butter Pastry

Sift flour once again with the salt into a bowl. Cut in the butter, rubbing it until it resembles fine crumbs; stir in just enough water to form a ball of dough. Cover with another bowl or a piece of plastic wrap, and let stand for at least 15 minutes.

Roll out as thinly as possible on a lightly floured board. Cut into appropriately sized circles.

Mini-Wiener Buns

32 appetizers

Preheat the oven to 400° F.

Cut the buns lengthwise with a sharp knife; then halve the rolls, but do not cut all the way through. Place the 16 pieces side by side in a 13-inch by 9-inch baking pan.

In a medium-sized non-stick skillet, fry the onion and bacon until the color begins to change; add the sauerkraut, brown sugar, dill, and caraway seeds if you are using them. Fry together for 10-15 minutes.

Put a spoonful of the sauerkraut mixture into each roll half, top with wiener, then another spoonful of sauerkraut to make sandwiches. Bake for 15 minutes. Carefully cut the 16 roll halves into 2 pieces each, making 32 appetizers. Serve hot.

8 white or brown hotdog rolls

1 onion, chopped

2 bacon strips, diced

2 cups sauerkraut, well drained

2 Tbsp brown sugar

$1/2$ tsp chopped dill

$1/2$ tsp caraway seeds (optional)

8 wieners

Corned Beef Sauerkraut Balls

60 balls

These appetizers can be prepared, cooked, and frozen ahead of time. To serve, thaw, and heat them in a 400 F oven for 15 minutes.

Grind sauerkraut, beef, onion, and crackers together. Mix well. Add egg, sugar, and flour. Mix thoroughly. Shape into one-inch balls. Fry in oil at 375° F until lightly browned, about 1 minute. Drain on absorbent paper, and serve hot.

2 cups sauerkraut

12-oz tin corned beef

1 medium onion

12 crisp rye crackers

1 egg, slightly beaten

1 Tbsp sugar

$3/4$ cup all-purpose or unbleached flour

oil for frying

Sandwiches

Sandwiches

The addition of sauerkraut adds piquancy to an otherwise ordinary sandwich. You can serve these sandwiches hot or cold, toasted or plain. Try some of these variations of Reuben sandwiches — or you can create your own.

Cold Corned Beef Reuben

1 serving

2 slices rye bread

mustard or horseradish dressing to taste

2-3 Tbsp rinsed, drained sauerkraut

1 slice cold canned corned beef

Corned beef is a favorite served with sauerkraut. The simplest way of making a Reuben is to combine the two.

Spread rye bread with mustard or horseradish dressing; add a layer of sauerkraut and a slice of corned beef. Top with second slice of bread.

Hot Reuben

1 serving

2 slices rye bread

Thousand Island dressing

2-4 slices thin corned beef

2 Tbsp drained sauerkraut

1 slice Mozzarella cheese

butter

Some prefer a hot sandwich for lunch. Pumpernickel bread is also good with this one.

On one slice of bread spread Thousand Island dressing, and place a layer of corned beef, sauerkraut, and cheese. Cover with second slice of bread. Butter the outsides of the sandwich.

Grill, or place in a medium hot skillet, browning lightly on both sides.

Reuben Sandwiches

10-12 servings

Place corned beef, bay leaves, and cloves in a large, deep pot and cover with cold water. Bring water to a boil over moderate heat; reduce the heat, and simmer the corned beef for 2 ½ to 3 hours, or until tender. Add the sauerkraut and caraway in the last 30 minutes, so it can cook with the corned beef.

Remove the corned beef and sauerkraut from the cooking water, and drain both well. Set aside the sauerkraut; let the corned beef rest, covered, for about 10 minutes.

For each sandwich, toast two slices of the rye bread; butter each slice. Place two or three slices of corned beef on the buttered side of one slice, and top with a layer of sauerkraut, and a slice of cheese. Broil to melt the cheese, then cover with the second slice of toast. Serve immediately.

Variation: Mix sour cream and onion dip mix thoroughly; spread on a second slice of toast before serving.

2 ½ to 3 lb raw corned beef

2 bay leaves

3 whole cloves

3 cups sauerkraut

½ tsp caraway seeds (optional)

20-24 slices rye bread

butter

20-24 slices Swiss or Cheddar cheese

Creamy Onion Jumbos

6 servings

Put the sauerkraut in a medium-sized pan. Wrap the corned beef lightly in foil wrap and place on top of the sauerkraut; cover the pan. Simmer for 10-15 minutes for the flavors to blend.

Stir the sour cream in a bowl and add the onion soup mix to taste. Spread this on one slice of bread. Place 3 slices of corned beef on top. Spoon the drained sauerkraut on top, dividing it evenly. Cover with the remaining slices of bread. Serve warm.

2-3 cups sauerkraut

12 thin slices corned beef

¾ cup sour cream

1 pkg onion soup mix or 2-3 Tbsp bulk onion soup mix, to taste

12 large slices rye bread

Kaiser Bun Reubens

2 cups drained sauerkraut

¹/₂ tsp caraway or dill seed

*¹/₄ tsp garlic powder or
1 garlic clove, minced*

*6 kaiser or whole wheat
buns*

butter or margarine

12 thin slices corned beef

*¹/₂ cup Russian or favourite
dressing*

6 slices Cheddar cheese

Preheat the toaster oven or grill. Toss the sauerkraut with the dill or caraway seed and the garlic. Set aside.

Split the buns in half. Lightly butter both halves. Spread the dressing on one half; top with 2 slices corned beef, the kraut mixture and a slice of cheese. Place all the bun halves in a toaster or grill until the cheese melts and the buns slightly toasted. Remove and top the cheese with the bun halves. Serve warm.

4 servings

Sauerkraut Beef Plate

*3 cups drained and chopped
sauerkraut*

*1 cup or more Thousand
Island dressing*

*8 large slices pumpernickel
bread, buttered*

*¹/₂ lb sliced Muenster or
Swiss cheese*

*8 slices canned or fresh
cooked corned beef*

dill pickles, sliced

*spiced crabapples or 8 slices
fried apples*

Garnished with dill pickle slices and rosy pickled crabapples or some fried apple slices, this makes a hearty and handsome lunch dish.

Put the sauerkraut into a bowl and moisten with the dressing.

Place one slice of bread on each of 4 plates; top each slice with cheese, then corned beef. Spoon sauerkraut over the beef, then cover with remaining slices of bread. Cut each sandwich in half. Place a slice of dill pickle on each and hold in place with a toothpick.

Garnish with spiced crabapples or two fried apple slices.

Poppy Seed Reubens

6-8 servings

In a small bowl, mix together the first four ingredients until the sugar is dissolved.

In a medium-sized bowl, place the sauerkraut, the chopped onion, and the chili peppers. Pour over the vinegar, sugar, oil sauce, and mix well to blend. Let stand a minimum of one hour. Drain well.

Split the rolls, and spread each piece lightly with butter or margarine. Put about 2 Tbsp sauerkraut mixture on each slice of corned beef; roll each slice tightly, jelly-roll fashion. Place 3 meat rolls on the bottom half of each bun. Cover with the remaining half. Slice to serve.

¹/₄ cup cider vinegar

¹/₄ cup sugar

3 Tbsp vegetable oil

salt and pepper to taste

6 cups drained sauerkraut, or sauerkraut and fresh cabbage mixed

1 onion chopped

2-3 red chili peppers, finely chopped

4 large poppy seed rolls

butter or margarine

12 thin slices corned beef

Reuben Hamburger

1 serving

Hamburger lends itself to many uses and can be combined with many flavors. This little sandwich is the simplest and can be prepared in a hurry.

Cook the hamburger patty in a non-stick skillet. When brown on one side, turn over and place a slice of cheese on the cooked side. Top with onion slices and sauerkraut. Cook until cheese begins to melt. Lift and put into the prepared bun.

1 hamburger patty

1 slice Mozzarella or caraway cheese

2 thin slices onion

1-2 Tbsp drained sauerkraut

1 hamburger bun, split and toasted

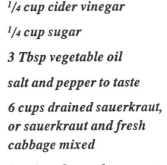

Parcelled Hamburgers

1 lb lean ground beef or lean
ground pork

1 tsp salt

pepper to taste

1 tsp dry mustard

1 clove garlic, minced

1 tsp dried dillweed

$^{1}/_{2}$ cup drained sauerkraut

8 slices bacon

8 slices pumpernickel bread

butter

Preheat broiler.

Mix the ground beef with the salt, pepper, mustard, garlic, and dillweed. Make 8 patties about $^{1}/_{2}$ inch thick. Place about 2 Tbsp sauerkraut on each of the 4 patties; top with the other 4 patties.

Wrap 2 slices of bacon around each parcel and secure with a toothpick. Broil about 6 minutes on each side, about 4 inches from the heat source or until the meat is medium-done and the bacon is crisp. Serve between 2 slices of pumpernickel bread.

Layered Reubens

$^{3}/_{4}$ cup mayonnaise or
Miracle Whip Dressing

$^{1}/_{4}$ cup hot chili sauce

1 Tbsp chopped parsley

12 slices rye bread

2 medium tomatoes, sliced

8 slices caraway cheese,
halved

2 medium onions, sliced

8 thin slices corned beef

2 cups drained sauerkraut

Chili sauce and caraway cheese added to the sauerkraut give these 3-decker sandwiches a flavor all their own.

Preheat oven to 400° F.

Combine the mayonnaise or Miracle Whip Dressing with the chili sauce and the parsley. Spread on each slice as the sandwiches are made.

Layer the sandwiches in this way:
- Top one slice of bread with tomato, cheese, and onion.
- Top second slice of bread with corned beef, and sauerkraut. Place remaining slice of bread on top of the sauerkraut, spread side down.

Cut each sandwich in half, then wrap loosely in foil. Place on a cookie sheet and bake for 20 minutes, or until heated through. Serve hot.

Smoked Sausage Reubens

4 servings

Corned beef combines well with sauerkraut, and so do other meats and poultry. Sausages and apples are used in this very tasty luncheon dish. I prefer to use Bavarian smokies, but you could substitute wieners in their place.

Put the sausages into a small saucepan and cover them with cold water. Bring to a boil, then simmer for 3-4 minutes. Drain well to remove much of the fat. Set aside.

Combine the sauerkraut with apple and sugar in a medium-size pan; heat to boiling. Cover. Simmer for 15 minutes to blend flavors. Drain.

Split the sausages in half lengthwise. Using a medium-sized skillet, sauté them in butter or margarine.

Blend the dressing with the chili sauce, add the minced onion, grate and add the cheese. Place 2 slices of bread on each of 4 serving plates. Spread each slice with part of the dressing mix. Layer sauerkraut, remaining dressing, and the sausages. Garnish with parsley. Serve with pickles of your choice.

3/4 lb smoked sausage links

3-4 cups drained sauerkraut

1 large or 2 small tart apples, cored and diced

3 Tbsp sugar

butter or margarine

1/2 cup mayonnaise or Miracle Whip Dressing

1/2 cup chili sauce

2 Tbsp finely chopped onion

1/2 to 1 cup Cheddar cheese

8 large slices caraway rye bread

parsley

Country Reubens

1 ¹/₂ lb pork sausage meat

sage, savory, oregano, thyme, Italian seasoning or a pinch of cayenne

5-6 Tbsp water

1 medium onion, chopped

1-2 Tbsp butter

2 strips bacon, diced

1 cup drained sauerkraut

¹/₂ tsp caraway or dill seed

6 hamburger buns

6 slices Swiss cheese

slices of pimiento-stuffed olives

plate of assorted raw vegetables

corn or potato chips, or nachos

Burgers never looked better nor tasted so good with a blend of cheese, sauerkraut, and sausage. Excellent fare for an impromptu party.

Preheat broiler.

Season the sausage meat to your taste. Form into 6 patties. Put in a skillet with the water and cover tightly. Simmer for 5-6 minutes; then drain off the water to remove some of the fat. Cook patties until browned and well done.

In heavy-bottomed, medium-sized pan, melt the butter; add the onions, and bacon. Cook lightly until the onions are soft and the bacon is translucent. Add the sauerkraut and seeds. Cook slowly, stirring frequently to prevent browning.

Split and toast the buns. Put a slice of cheese on each patty and broil until the cheese begins to melt. Place 2-3 Tbsp of sauerkraut on bottom half of each bun. Put the patty and cheese on top of the sauerkraut. Spread a few olive slices on top before covering with the other half of the bun. Serve hot with the raw vegetables and an assortment of chips.

Devilled Ham Reubens

2 servings

Ham and cheese are a favorite combination for sandwiches. Add a bit of sauerkraut and—voila—a new kind of sandwich! Just great!

Place half the cheese on two slices of bread, spread with devilled ham; top the ham with sauerkraut and remaining cheese slices, then the bread.

Butter the outsides of both sandwiches. Put into a 10-inch non-stick skillet and cover tightly. Brown one side and the other, cooking slowly until the cheese melts.

Cut the sandwiches in half and arrange on two plates. Garnish with one or two lettuce leaves, placing the wedges of tomato and cucumber slices on the lettuce.

4 slices Cheddar or Swiss cheese

4 slices rye bread

1 small can of devilled ham

1/2 cup drained sauerkraut

butter or margarine

lettuce leaves for garnish

tomato wedges

cucumber slices

Turkey or Chicken Reuben

4 servings

Turkey breast is used in these delicious sandwiches, together with hot mustard, Miracle Whip Dressing, and sauerkraut. But chicken breast, or if you prefer, the dark meat, will taste equally well. Some chopped celery is nice in this.

Set out the 8 slices of bread in pairs; butter 4 slices.

Mix the sauerkraut and the dressing in a small bowl. Spread about 1½ Tbsp of sauerkraut mixture on each of the 4 buttered bread slices. Cover with slices of turkey, then top each one with one slice of cheese.

Spread the remaining 4 slices of bread with the hot mustard and top the cheese, mustard side down, to complete the sandwiches. Serve cold.

8 slices bread

butter or margarine

2 cups drained sauerkraut

3/4 cup Miracle Whip Salad Dressing

turkey slices

4 slices Swiss or Cheddar cheese

Reuben Turnovers

1 cup drained sauerkraut

¹/₄ tsp dill seed

2 Tbsp sour cream

2 Tbsp Miracle Whip Salad Dressing

1 Tbsp chopped green pepper

1 Tbsp chopped green onion

1 Tbsp chili sauce

1 pkg refrigerated crescent rolls (8 rolls)

1 cup minced ham

¹/₂ cup shredded American, Swiss, or Cheddar cheese

¹/₂ cup drained sauerkraut, chopped

1 cup chopped corned beef

¹/₂ cup shredded Swiss cheese

1 Tbsp chopped green onion

1 Tbsp chopped fresh parsley

Turnovers are a great way to serve freshly baked crescent rolls. Use a package of refrigerated crescent rolls or make your own.

Snip the sauerkraut into fine pieces. Combine with the dill seed, sour cream, Miracle Whip Salad Dressing, green and red pepper, green onion, and the chili sauce. Mix well and set aside.

Unroll the crescent roll dough and form into 9 rectangles 6 inches by 3 ¹/₂ inches by pressing edges together. Spoon some chopped ham onto half of each rectangle. Top with the sauerkraut mixture and cheese. Fold over the other half of dough, seal edges with the tines of a fork. Place on an ungreased baking sheet. Bake until golden brown, about 10 minutes.

Variations: For spicier turnovers, add a pinch of cayenne, or you can experiment with the following fillings:

Corned Beef Filling

Mix the sauerkraut and the corned beef. Combine with the remaining ingredients.

Wiener Filling

Combine the wieners and the sauerkraut. Add the pickle and mustard. Mix well.

4 wieners, minced

$^1/_2$ cup drained sauerkraut, chopped

$^1/_2$ cup chopped sweet pickle

1 Tbsp dry mustard

Spicy Beef Filling

Cut the meat in very thin slices. Then cut the slices into $^1/_4$-inch strips. Brown quickly in a skillet, using a little olive or vegetable oil. Cook the peppers and onions until soft, then add the tomato and sauerkraut. Remove and set aside. Combine the $^1/_4$ cup cold water and the remaining ingredients and add to the meat. Cook and stir until bubbly. Stir in the pepper, onion, sauerkraut and tomato mixture. Heat through.

$^1/_2$ lb round steak

1 Tbsp olive or vegetable oil

$^1/_2$ green pepper, chopped

2 Tbsp chopped green onion

$^1/_2$ cup chopped tomato

$^1/_2$ cup drained sauerkraut

$^1/_4$ cup cold water

2 Tbsp cornstarch

$^1/_4$ tsp curry powder

$^1/_4$ tsp ground ginger

1-2 Tbsp soy sauce

$^1/_2$ tsp sugar

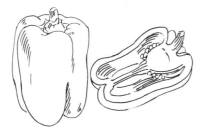

Prairie Hot Dog

4 servings

4 barbecue wieners

4 strips bacon

1 cup drained sauerkraut

chopped onion, fried or raw

1/4 cup mayonnaise

4 hot dog buns

butter or margarine

mustard

Hot dogs can be as varied as you wish. They are great enhanced with sauerkraut and bacon.

Wrap each wiener with a strip of bacon. Fry gently in a skillet over medium heat, turning it often until the bacon is done and the wieners are hot.

Chop the sauerkraut, add fried or raw onion, and mix with the mayonnaise. Split the buns lengthwise, toast lightly, and butter. Spread with a layer of sauerkraut, place a hot wiener on top, and spread with mustard. Serve hot.

Wiener Reuben Sandwiches

8 servings

2-3 cups drained sauerkraut, chopped finely

1/2 cup minced onion

8 wieners

mustard

4 slices Swiss cheese, quartered in strips

8 hot dog buns

Thousand Island Dressing

Adding cheese and Thousand Island dressing makes this a delightfully different hot dog. For a spicier taste use Bavarian smokies.

Preheat broiler. Mix the sauerkraut and onion together. Slit the wieners in half lengthwise. Spread with sauerkraut. Broil about 3-4 inches below the heat source for about 5 minutes, until the sauerkraut is hot. Top with the cheese strips and broil until the cheese melts. Toast the split buns. Spread the dressing on one half and mustard on the other. Put the wieners in the buns. Serve immediately.

Veggie Delight Sandwich with Soda Bread

4 servings

Soda Bread

Preheat oven to 375° F. Grease a 6-inch rounf pan. In a small bowl, combine vinegar and milk; set aside. Combine the flours and baking soda. Cut in the butter until it makes coarse crumbs. Stir in the milk mixture, mustard, and scallions. Turn out on a lightly floured surface and knead 5 minutes until smooth. Shape into a 6-inch round loaf. Place in greased pan and bake 45-50 minutes or until the crust is brown and loaf is hollow-sounding when tapped. Cool at least 10 minutes.

1 Tbsp apple cider vinegar

2/3 cup milk

1 1/4 cup whole wheat flour

3/4 cup all purpose flour

1 tsp baking soda

2 tbsp butter or margarine

1/4 cup prepared mustard

4 scallions, chopped.

Filling

In a large bowl combine all ingredients except the corned beef. Mix well. Slice the bread horizontally in half. Place the corned beef on the bottom half of the bread. Spoon sauerkraut on top of the meat. Top with the other slice of bread. Cut in 4 portions. Serve warm with dill pickles and sharp mustard.

Variation: Use large baking powder biscuits instead of soda bread.

2 1/2 cups drained sauerkraut

1 Tbsp dill seed

1/2 tsp salt

1/4 tsp pepper

1/2 cup alfalfa sprouts (optional)

1 medium carrot, grated

1/2 cup sour cream

1/3 cup apple cider vinegar

3/4 lb sliced corned beef

Salads

Salads

While we were quite young, my sister and I liked to hang around the kitchen, eager to know what was being prepared and wanting to taste everything our mother made. Once in while, she took a dish full of fresh sauerkraut out of the barrel, drained it, and put it on the table as a side dish. We always wanted a taste before supper. Sometimes she gave us a mouthful each, and at other times, a handful with the admonition to "disappear for a while."

Sauerkraut, especially when it has just fermented, has a sweet- sour, cool taste. It does not need to be rinsed at this time and makes excellent cold salads.

Sauerkraut as a Side Dish

Take as large a bowlful as you need. If it is newly fermented, sauerkraut needs to be drained only slightly, but if it is very sour, it should be rinsed in cold water first, then drained. Serve it as is, or dress it up as a salad.

One of the simplest ways of dressing up a dish of sauerkraut is to add a bit of oil and vinegar. Your favorite vinaigrette would be fine. A similar salad is made with slight variations in Germany, Poland, and Ukraine. In France, the sauerkraut is boiled with onions, drained, then tossed lightly with oil, vinegar, salt and pepper. It is piled in a bowl and decorated with sliced boiled eggs and/or sliced cooked vegetables.

Sauerkraut Salad

6-8 servings

My mother used to add a bit of sugar to this salad.

Put all ingredients into a bowl. Moisten with vinegar. Toss and serve.

5 cups drained sauerkraut

salt to taste

2 apples, peeled, cored, and chopped

3 Tbsp salad oil

2 Tbsp minced onion

1-2 carrots, diced

2-3 Tbsp vinegar

Polish Salad

4-6 servings

Partially drain the sauerkraut. Mix in all the other ingredients, adding sufficient sugar and lemon to give the sauerkraut a sweet and sour flavor. Stir together well. Serve chilled.

2 1/2 cups sauerkraut

3/4 Tbsp olive oil

salt and pepper to taste

lemon juice to taste

1 apple, peeled, cored, shredded

1 tsp sugar

Salad from Ukraine

1 onion, chopped

1 green pepper, chopped

1 tsp sugar

salt and pepper, to taste

3 Tbsp salad oil

parsley

paprika

Rinse the sauerkraut in cold water if necessary. Drain well. Chop it coarsely and mix with the remaining ingredients. Add salt if needed. Chill before serving. Garnish with parsley and paprika.

Hot Sauerkraut Salad

If you prefer a hot salad you can follow the French style (see index) or you can follow this recipe.

Use the recipe for Polish or Ukrainian Salad, but omit the oil. Mix the ingredients well. Preheat a skillet and add 3 Tbsp melted butter or some bacon drippings; add other ingredients. Stir until well heated. Add a bit more butter if needed.

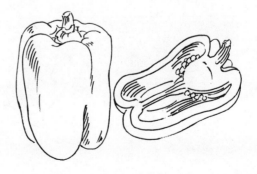

Polskie Salat

Drain the sauerkraut and reserve the juice. In a large bowl, combine the sauerkraut, onions, and hard-cooked eggs. Put the rest of the ingredients in a jar, cover, and shake vigorously until well blended.

Add this dressing to the sauerkraut. Toss lightly to blend all ingredients.

Assorted vegetables can be added to the sauerkraut. Wine vinegar gives a subtle flavor not found in white vinegar, which may also be used.

4 cups sauerkraut

1/2 cup chopped green onions

3 hard-cooked eggs, chopped

1 tsp dry mustard

pepper to taste

1/3 cup salad oil

1/3 cup sauerkraut juice

2 Tbsp sugar

2 Tbsp wine vinegar

Piquant Salad

10 servings

Some like it "hot." There's nothing like some hot peppers to give Sauerkraut Salad that extra bite! This salad is especially good with barbecued meals.

Rinse the sauerkraut if necessary. Add peppers, onion, pimiento, celery, and carrot. Mix well.

To make the dressing, boil together for 1 minute water, vinegar, sugar, salt and pepper to taste. Let cool. Pour over the sauerkraut mixture and let stand for several hours before using. The longer this stands, the better it gets. It will keep a long time if refrigerated.

Variations:

- If you do not like hot peppers, omit them and use a sweet red pepper to give the salad color.
- Instead of water, add a *1/2* cup of oil.
- Use your favorite vinaigrette dressing instead of the dressing suggested.

3 cups drained sauerkraut

1 green pepper, chopped

1 red hot pepper, chopped pimiento, or pinch of cayenne

1 large onion, chopped

1 cup diced celery

1 cup grated carrot

1/2 cup water 5 Tbsp

1/2 cup vinegar

1 cup sugar

salt and pepper to taste

Pennsylvania Dutch Salad

3 cups drained sauerkraut, chopped

³/₄ cup shredded carrots

¹/₈ tsp mustard seed

3 Tbsp salad oil

2 tsp sugar

salt and pepper to taste

1 onion, chopped

³/₄ cup chopped green pepper

³/₄ cup chopped red pepper

¹/₈ tsp celery seed

3 Tbsp chili sauce (hot if you like it)

This salad is named for the Pennsylvania Dutch who are famous for their excellent food. This pretty and tasty salad has been adapted from their cuisine.

Put all the ingredients into a serving dish. Mix well, and refrigerate for several hours before serving.

Ham and Sauerkraut Salad

¹/₂ lb grapes

1 unpeeled apple, diced

1 cup cooked ham, julienned

2 ¹/₂ cups drained sauerkraut, rinsed if necessary

³/₄ cup yogurt or sour cream

1 ¹/₂ tsp liquid honey

salt and pepper to taste

Fruit is a great addition to sauerkraut, enhancing the sweet-sour flavor. This simple salad combines some unusual ingredients.

Wash the grapes, cut in half and remove the seeds. Mix well with the apple, ham, and sauerkraut.

Combine the yogurt, honey, salt and pepper, and mix well. Marinate for 15-20 minutes to blend the flavors. Pour over the sauerkraut mixture.

Ham Salad

4 servings

Ham and pineapple combinations are used in a number of dishes. Here is an unusual salad combining ham and pineapple with sauerkraut.

Toss the sauerkraut lightly. Drain the pineapple, reserving the juice, and chop the slices into small pieces. Mix the pineapple and diced ham with the sauerkraut. You can put the cherries in with the salad or you can reserve them to scatter over the top for color.

In a small saucepan, heat the pineapple juice over low heat. When it's simmering, add the honey, stirring until dissolved. Stir in the oil and lemon juice. Pour over the salad.

3 cups drained sauerkraut, drained if necessary

5 slices canned pineapple

1 lb cooked, diced ham

$^1/_2$ cup glazed or maraschino cherries (optional)

8 Tbsp canned pineapple juice

1 Tbsp honey

2 Tbsp vegetable oil

3 Tbsp lemon juice

Beet and Potato Salad

6-8 servings

A very different version of a potato salad may appear at a Polish table. Here is an interesting blend of potatoes, beets, other vegetables, and a tangy dressing.

Cook 4-5 small beets until tender. Let cool before peeling and dicing. Chop the sauerkraut; mix with the other vegetables in a bowl.

Combine the oil, vinegar, mustard, pickles, salt and pepper. Stir to blend and pour over the salad. Mix well. Refrigerate for at least two hours before serving. Serve sprinkled with the chopped parsley, fresh dill, or both.

4-5 small beets

3 cups drained sauerkraut

$^1/_4$ cup chopped celery

$^1/_2$ cup chopped green onion

2 cups cooked, diced potatoes

$^1/_3$ cup salad oil

2 Tbsp cider vinegar

2 Tbsp prepared sharp mustard

2 Tbsp minced gherkins, or sweet pickle

salt and pepper to taste

3 Tbsp chopped fresh parsley, or dill leaves

Potato Sauerkraut Salad

4-5 medium potatoes

2 ¹/₂ cups drained sauerkraut

¹/₂ cup chopped green
onions with tops

¹/₂ cup chopped celery

¹/₄ cup salad oil

2 Tbsp cider vinegar

2 tsp sugar

¹/₂ tsp caraway or dill seed

pepper to taste

1 large carrot, grated

From Czechoslovakia, we get this version of a zesty potato salad. It is made colorful with celery, carrots, and green onions.

Scrub the potatoes and boil them in their jackets until tender. Peel and slice while still warm. Place in a bowl.

Add the sauerkraut to the potatoes along with the onions and celery.

Mix together the oil, vinegar, sugar and seasonings. Pour over the vegetables and mix well to blend the flavors. Sprinkle the top with grated carrot.

4-6 servings

Savory Fruit Salad

3 cups drained sauerkraut

2 large apples, cored,thinly
sliced

1 large pear or 2 small,
cored, and thinly sliced

1 cup red seedless grapes

1 medium onion, chopped

juice of 1 lemon

salt to taste

¹/₂ tsp sugar

4 Tbsp cranberry sauce

A fruit salad to serve with barbecued or stuffed spare ribs, Savory Fruit Salad is a nice combination of sauerkraut and fruit dressed up with cranberry sauce and lemon. You can add other fruit such as pineapple or papaya to create your own favorite.

Place tossed sauerkraut in a bowl. Cut grapes in half if they are large, and add them with the apples and pears to the sauerkraut. Add chopped onion. Mix to blend.

In a small bowl, beat together the lemon juice, salt, and sugar. Pour over the salad. Stir, cover, and let stand for at least 30 minutes. Stir in the cranberry sauce just before serving.

Tomato-Sauerkraut Cups

6 servings

These are pretty enough to grace a dinner table. Stuffed tomatoes always look great, but these have a different, surprise filling.

Pat the sauerkraut dry between sheets of paper towels. Chop coarsely and place in a bowl. Add the chopped celery and onion.

Wash the tomatoes and cut off the tops; scoop out the insides with a teaspoon. Turn the tomatoes upside down to drain; then chill. Chop the pulp and add to the sauerkraut mixture.

Combine the rest of the ingredients in a cup. Stir well. Pour over the sauerkraut mixture; toss lightly to blend. Let stand at least 30 minutes.

To serve, line serving plates with the shredded lettuce. Stuff the cups with the sauerkraut mixture and place on a bed of lettuce.

2 cups drained sauerkraut

1/2 cup chopped celery

1 medium onion, chopped

6 medium, firm, ripe tomatoes

3 Tbsp salad oil

2 tsp chopped pimiento (optional)

1 Tbsp cider vinegar

1 Tbsp catsup

1 tsp sugar

1/2 tsp Worcestershire sauce

shredded lettuce

Jellied Sauerkraut

4-5 servings

Jellied salads are a pleasant change from the regular kinds of salads. This one is versatile and can be combined with other ingredients. Be brave and experiment!

Chop the sauerkraut finely. Mix the jelly according to instructions and let it set until partially jelled. Stir in the sauerkraut, celery and onions. Refrigerate until well set.

Variations:
- 1/2 cup chopped or julienned ham
- 1/2 cup grated carrot
- 1/2 cup diced red or green pepper
- A fruit cup consisting of 1 apple (diced), 1 pear (diced), 1/2 cups seedless green grapes, diced tomatoes

2 1/2 cups drained sauerkraut

1 pkg lime or lemon-lime jelly powder

1/4 cup diced celery

1/3 cup chopped green onions with tops

Beet and Avocado
with Sauerkraut

6 servings

1 lb young beets

2 ¹/₂ cups drained sauerkraut

¹/₂ cup chopped green
onions

¹/₃ cup diced celery

1 cup chopped, cooked ham

¹/₂ lb Chinese cabbage or
Boston lettuce

2 large ripe avocados

2 medium red onions, peeled
and sliced thinly

1 cup bean sprouts

ripe or stuffed olives

sliced dill pickles

pickled eggs

2 tsp dry mustard

2 tsp minced garlic

2 Tbsp soy sauce

¹/₂ tsp black pepper

3 Tbsp lemon juice

2 ¹/₄ cups olive oil

*A festive dish suitable for the most distinguished table;
or a gourmet lunch to tickle the palate, this combines
avocados with beets, bean sprouts, and other good things.*

Scrub the beets and place them in a pot with water to
cover. Boil until tender. Drain and cool enough to
handle. Peel them; cut into julienne strips. Set aside.

Rinse the sauerkraut if needed. Drain well. Put into a
bowl and add the green onion, the celery, and ham. Mix
well and put into the refrigerator to chill.

To assemble, select a large platter. Arrange the
Chinese cabbage or lettuce leaves on it. Break the leaves
into pieces and put the most attractive pieces around the
edges. Arrange the fluffed-out sauerkraut mixture in the
centre, leaving a 2-inch margin showing.

Halve the avocados; remove the pits, and peel. Cut
each half into 6 lengthwise slices. Divide them and the
beets into 6 equal portions. Arrange alternately around
the platter on top of the sauerkraut. Separate the onions
into rings and scatter around the edges. Top the onion
rings with the bean sprouts. Pour the salad dressing
(recipe follows) over the salad, lightly coating all the
ingredients.

Garnish with ripe or stuffed olives, pickles or pickled
eggs.

Dressing

In a medium-sized bowl, prepare the dressing by
combining the mustard, minced garlic, soy sauce, pepper,
and lemon juice. Whisk together; then, in a slow, steady
stream, pour in the olive oil, whisking constantly until
the dressing is smooth and thick.

Garlic Sausage Salad

4 servings

Most smoked sausages go well with sauerkraut. This one is with garlic sausage, but you may use knackwurst or kielbasa.

Place sausage in a pan of warm water, bring to a boil, reduce heat, and simmer for 5-6 minutes. Set sausage aside. When cool, remove casing and slice thinly. Next, mix apples and lemon juice.

Add the sausage, pickle, onion, pepper, dill, caraway, and apples to the sauerkraut. Combine the sugar and oil with 1/4 tsp salt, if needed. Mix into the salad. Chill for several hours before using.

1 1/4 lb garlic sausage

2 medium apples, peeled, cored, chopped

2 Tbsp lemon juice

1/2 cup diced dill pickle

salt if needed

1 small onion, chopped

1/2 cup chopped green pepper

1 tsp dillweed

1/2 tsp caraway seeds (optional)

2 1/2 cups sauerkraut

3 Tbsp sugar

2 Tbsp salad oil

Smoked Fish Salad

3 cups drained sauerkraut, coarsely chopped

1 medium red pepper, julienned

1 medium green pepper, julienned

1 large apple- diced

1 large pear, diced

juice of 1 lemon

7-oz can oil-packed tuna

12 pimiento-stuffed olives

³/₄ lb smoked fish

¹/₂ cup chopped celery

¹/₂ cup green onions, chopped

¹/₂ tsp sugar

¹/₄ cup salad oil

salt and pepper to taste

Smoked fish is nice by itself, but you can dress it up with vegetables and fruit to make an excellent salad. Use your favorite smoked fish.

In a large bowl, combine sauerkraut, peppers, apple, pear, and sprinkle the fruit with a teaspoon of the lemon juice to prevent discoloration, reserving the rest of the juice. Drain the tuna, reserving the oil. Break the tuna into small pieces and add to the sauerkraut mixture.

Halve the olives and cut the smoked fish into bite-sized pieces. Add these to the salad, together with the celery and green onions.

Beat together the tuna oil, the salad oil, and the rest of the lemon juice. Add the salt and pepper. Stir into the salad. Cover and let stand 35-45 minutes before serving.

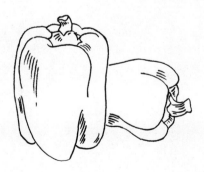

Soups

Soups

Soups made with sauerkraut are usually thick and filling. They may be made with meat stocks — pork, beef, poultry — or a vegetable stock. My own preference is pork stock, but I have used other meat stocks, which are just as tasty.

When I make a sauerkraut soup, I don't serve anything else with it other than rye bread. The soup goes well with any kind of rye bread, light or dark, with or without caraway, or with any of the black breads such as pumpernickel.

It is important to check the saltiness and strength of the sauerkraut before adding salt to the soup. You can reduce the sharpness of strong-flavored sauerkraut by rinsing it with cold water before use, but rinsing may wash away some of the good taste. Another and, perhaps, a better way, is to add some shredded fresh cabbage to the soup.

Many of these soups depend on long, slow cooking to develop their full flavor, although there are those that can be ready in a short time.

Sauerkraut Soup

6 servings

Potatoes are often added to sauerkraut soups. This one is simple to make. It is economical, too, as it uses bones and beef flank for the stock.

Brown the meat and onion in the cooking oil in a large soup pot. Add the sauerkraut, along with the seasonings, and the water. Bring to a boil, reduce heat, and simmer for 2 hours, adding more water if necessary. Remove the meat and let it cool. Add the potatoes to the stock and cook until they are tender, about 20 minutes. Cut up the cooled meat and put it back into the soup. Reheat, and serve hot.

1 1/2 lb beef flank and bones

1 1/2 cups chopped onion

1 Tbsp cooking oil

2 1/2 cups drained sauerkraut

salt to taste

1/2 tsp pepper

3 bay leaves

3 whole cloves (optional)

2 qts water

1 1/2 cups cubed potatoes

Sweet and Sour Soup

4-6 servings

Here is a different version of a very simple soup. It is sweetened with sugar and allspice.

Cut the meat into serving-size pieces. Put the meat in a large pot and cover completely with cold water. Bring to a boil, skim, then add the spices and sugar; simmer for about 2 hours. Rinse the sauerkraut if necessary, and add it and the vegetable juice to the pan; return to the boil, reduce heat and allow to simmer for an hour or so until the meat is very tender. Serve with creamed, mashed potatoes, or rice as a side dish.

3 lbs brisket or lean beef ribs

1 tsp powdered allspice

1/2 tsp pepper

4 whole cloves

salt to taste

3 bay leaves

2 Tbsp brown sugar

4 cups drained sauerkraut

2 cups vegetable juice

Soup from Alsace

4 slices bacon, diced

4 cups drained sauerkraut

1 onion, finely chopped

³/₄ Tbsp flour

8 cups beef stock (optional)

1 apple, peeled, grated

¹/₂ tsp caraway seeds

salt and pepper to taste

¹/₂ cup white wine

From Alsace we have a soup flavored with bacon, apple, and caraway.

Fry diced bacon in a 2-quart saucepan. Rinse the sauerkraut if needed and drain well again. When the bacon is rendered, add the sauerkraut and onion to the hot fat and fry gently until they begin to brown slightly. Stir in the flour. Add the beef stock, stirring constantly, then the apple and seasonings. Simmer for about 10 minutes to blend. Check the seasonings and add wine if you wish. Serve hot.

One-Hour Soup

4 ¹/₂ cups drained sauerkraut

1 large onion, chopped

1 apple, peeled, grated

2 tsp sweet paprika

8 cups beef stock

2 bay leaves

6-oz can tomato paste

¹/₂ tsp caraway seeds

Cooking soup with meat is not strictly necessary but some good meat stock certainly helps the flavor. This interesting soup is flavored with tomato and paprika. Although I prefer to simmer my soups for much more than an hour, this recipe provides a nutritious meal in a relatively short time.

Rinse the sauerkraut if needed; drain well. Put all the ingredients in a pot; bring to a boil; reduce heat and simmer 45-60 minutes.

One-Hour Soup, Russian Style

6-8 servings

Here is another One-Hour Soup made with more vegetables and different herbs. It is quick and tasty.

Melt the butter in a large saucepan. Cook the onion, carrots, and celery until they become slightly colored. Add the potato. Stir in the flour. When smooth, add tomato pure and the sauerkraut. Cook for a few minute stirring constantly. Add the soup stock and the herbs. Bring to a boil, reduce heat, then simmer for 45-50 minutes. Season to taste. Serve hot with one or two teaspoons of sour cream in each soup dish.

4 Tbsp butter

1 onion, sliced

2 carrots, thinly sliced

1/4 cup chopped celery

1 large potato, peeled and sliced

3 Tbsp all purpose flour

1 Tbsp tomato pure

3 cups drained sauerkraut

6-8 cups beef stock

1 tsp chopped chervil

1 Tbsp chopped fresh parsley

sour cream

Anna's Sauerkraut Soup

4 cups drained sauerkraut

1-2 Tbsp butter

1 onion, chopped

2 ½ lb garlic sausage, sliced in ¼-inch rounds

6 cups beef stock

1 cup dry white wine

1 tsp caraway or dill seeds

2 bay leaves

3 whole cloves

salt and pepper to taste

The addition of wine adds a delicate bouquet to numerous dishes. If you like to cook with wine, it will enhance a sauerkraut soup. Flavor the soup with garlic sausage, herbs, and white wine.

Rinse the sauerkraut, if needed, and drain well. Melt the butter in a 6-8- quart saucepan and cook the onion in it until it is soft. Add the sausage and brown lightly. Add the stock, the wine, the sauerkraut, seeds, bay leaves, whole cloves, salt and pepper. Bring to a boil, reduce heat, and simmer, covered, for 30 or more minutes until the flavors are well blended. Add more water or wine if necessary. Remove the bay leaves and the whole cloves before serving.

Olives and Leeks Soup

2 leeks

2 celery stalks, chopped

¼ cup olive oil

paprika and black pepper, to taste

2 cups warm water

2 cups sauerkraut juice

⅓ cup raw rice, washed

15-20 ripe olives, pitted

2 eggs

Bulgarians combine olives with leeks and sauerkraut juice to make a unique soup.

Clean leeks and cut into fine rings. Wash the celery and cut into small pieces. In a skillet, fry both in oil until they turn golden. Sprinkle with paprika and pepper. Put into a 4-quart saucepan and add the water and sauerkraut juice. Cook gently for 15-20 minutes, then add washed rice and let simmer for another 20 minutes longer or until the rice is cooked. Slice the olives and add to the soup. Heat the soup well. Beat the eggs in a large bowl. Add to the soup slowly, stirring constantly so that the egg does not curdle. Correct the seasonings and serve.

Sharp Sauerkraut Soup

6-7 servings

Central Europe abounds in ways of making soup with sauerkraut. Each country has recipes with similar ingredients, but cooks use different herbs and vegetables to impart new flavors. This Hungarian soup utilizes very sour sauerkraut and tiny meatballs. It is a soup for those who like tangy, sharp flavors.

Put the sauerkraut in a saucepan. Add the water and bring to a boil. Reduce heat; simmer for 50 minutes. Drain and reserve the stock. In a Dutch oven, brown the onion and the garlic in the bacon fat. Add drained onion and garlic to the sausage meat; add the seasonings; form the sausage meat mixture into tiny balls, and brown, adding more fat if necessary. Return the stock to a boil. Remove the balls from the Dutch oven and add to the boiling stock. Brown the flour in the fat, gradually adding one cup of hot stock, stirring constantly. Add the rest of the soup. Combine with the sauerkraut. Heat to boiling and serve with 1 Tbsp or more of sour cream in each bowl and sliced rye bread or pumpernickel.

2 ¹/₂ cups very sour sauerkraut

6 cups water

1 large onion, chopped

1 clove garlic, finely minced

1 Tbsp bacon fat

2-3 tsp sweet paprika or to taste

³/₄ lb pork sausage meat

1-2 Tbsp all-purpose flour

salt and pepper to taste

sour cream

Two-in-One Soup

1 onion, chopped 1 carrot, thinly sliced 1 parsley root and top

1 parsnip, chopped

³/₄ cup chopped green onion

2 bunches assorted green herbs (parsley, dill, chervil, dried or fresh celery leaves)

5 cups water

1 small head lettuce, chopped

3 Tbsp raw rice

2 Tbsp cooking oil

¹/₂ cup sauerkraut juice

sour cream to taste

1 egg (optional)

salt and pepper to taste

Sauerkraut juice can be used to achieve a tangy flavor. This Romanian recipe creates a sour vegetable soup that can be served in two different ways.

Basic Soup

In a 6-8 quart pot, cook vegetables in water with half of the finely chopped green herbs. When the vegetables are tender, sprinkle the remaining herbs into the soup.

Serving Method One: In a small or medium-sized skillet, fry the rice in the cooking oil until golden in color. Add to the hot soup and boil slowly until tender. Add sauerkraut juice and stir. Serve with a dollop of sour cream. Add salt and pepper to taste.

Serving Method Two: Cook the rice separately. Beat the egg and combine with the sauerkraut juice. Add to the soup along with the cooked rice. Check the seasoning. Simmer slowly to heat. Serve with a spoonful or two of sour cream.

Sauerkraut Borscht

8-10 servings

To me, being raised in a Ukrainian home, the word "borscht" means beet soup, but to others from different countries it can mean a thick, hearty soup with cabbage, either fresh or fermented. It is hard to make just a little borscht!

Cut the bacon or ham into small pieces. Add to a 6 to 8-quart pot of water and bring to a boil. Simmer until the bacon is cooked, about 20 minutes. Tie the ginger, bay leaf, cloves, and garlic in cheesecloth and add to the broth with the sauerkraut and onions. Simmer slowly for another 20-30 minutes until the flavours are well blended. Add the parsley, dill, sugar, and tomatoes. Cook for another 10 minutes. Remove the cheesecloth with the herbs before serving.

Variation: To make Mennonite-style *borscht*, use brown sugar, and add cubed potatoes which have been boiled separately. At the last, add cream to taste. Delicious!

3 slices bacon, or ham

6 cups water or more

2 1/2 cups sauerkraut

4 onions, sliced

small piece of fresh ginger

1 bay leaf

2 whole cloves

1 clove garlic

1 Tbsp fresh parsley

1 Tbsp chopped dill

1/2 cup sugar

3 medium tomatoes, chopped

Sauerkraut as a Soup Garnish

Sauerkraut can be added to any soup. Unless it is mild-tasting, wash in cold water and dry the desired amount of sauerkraut. Put into a clear stock and cook gently. When cooked 20-30 minutes, drain and add to the soup.

Vegetable Soup with Sauerkraut

¹/₂ cup diced carrots

¹/₂ cup chopped green onion

¹/₂ cup chopped celery

two 10 ¹/₂-oz cans condensed beef consommé or 6 cups stock

¹/₂ cup uncooked rice

¹/₂ cup chopped green pepper

4 cups sauerkraut

4 cups stewed tomatoes or tomato juice

2 red chili peppers, dried, or to taste

Combine all the ingredients except the chili peppers in a large kettle. Bring to a boil, reduce heat, and simmer for about an hour until the vegetables are cooked. Add the chili peppers for the last 10 minutes. Remove the chili peppers from the pot. Serve the soup as is, or with a dollop of sour cream.

Mary's Sauerkraut Soup

So far, we have used soup stocks, butter, and cooking oil to give the soups richness, but meats in variety are used in the soups. Different cuts of beef may be used successfully. Here is a simple but tasty soup.

In a large saucepan or stock pot, cook the meat in the water until tender and the water has made good stock, adding the sauerkraut and onion in the last 45 minutes of cooking. Prepare a thin paste of the flour and water in a medium-sized bowl. When smooth, add the cream; then add all of the mixture to the soup, stirring constantly. Check the seasoning before serving.

The meat may be taken out and shredded or chopped before returning to the soup, or it may be sliced and served as a side dish.

This soup is made "to taste" and other ingredients may be added. You can put in more water, have a larger piece of meat, more or less sauerkraut, and more cream. The paste prevents the cream from curdling.

1 lb boiling beef, or any meaty cut

8 cups water

4 cups sauerkraut

1 onion, chopped

$1/2$ cup fresh parsley

3-4 Tbsp flour

$1/2$ cup water (approximately)

1 cup or more sweet cream

salt and pepper to taste

Ham and Wiener Soup

4 cups sauerkraut

3 bay leaves

6 cups beef broth

2 onions, chopped

3 slices bacon, diced

*1/2 cup tomato purée, or
2 Tbsp tomato paste*

1/2 tsp paprika

1/2 tsp caraway seeds

salt and pepper to taste

3 potatoes, peeled and grated

1/3 lb lean ham

4-6 wieners

A simple sauerkraut soup made different with the addition of ham and beef wieners. It can be ready in just over an hour.

Put the sauerkraut and the bay leaves in a medium-sized saucepan with 3 cups beef broth. Bring to a boil and simmer for 30 minutes. In a large non-stick skillet, fry the onions and bacon together until they are a golden color; then add to the sauerkraut together with 3 more cups of beef broth, the tomato purée or paste, the paprika, caraway seeds, and salt to taste. Soak the grated potatoes in cold water, press as dry as you can; add them too.

A few minutes before the soup is ready, dice the ham and the wieners and add them to the soup. Remove the bay leaves. Check the seasonings and serve.

Barley and Ribs Soup

6-8 servings

Adding some fresh cabbage to the sauerkraut cuts the tartness, leaving just a pleasant hint of sourness. A few vegetables and barley help to make a thick, tasty soup.

Cut the ribs into small pieces. In a medium-sized skillet, brown the ribs in some bacon drippings or oil. When they are well browned, remove them to the soup pot. Pour the vinegar into the drippings left in the pan, scraping the sides to loosen the brown bits; add to the pot. Add 1-2 Tbsp vegetable oil to the pan with the onions, dill or caraway, and bay leaves. Cook, stirring occasionally, until onion is soft—about 10 minutes. Put into the pot with the ribs. Add the stock, sauerkraut, shredded cabbage, carrots, tomatoes crushed in their own liquid, barley, and whole cloves. Bring to a boil, reduce heat, and simmer about 3 hours until the meat is falling off the bones. Skim, and discard fat from the soup. Correct the seasoning before serving.

3 ¹/₂ lb pork ribs

4 Tbsp bacon drippings, or vegetable oil, divided

3 Tbsp white wine vinegar

1 large onion, diced

1 tsp caraway or dill seeds

3 bay leaves

8 cups beef stock

2-4 cups sauerkraut

2 cups shredded green cabbage

¹/₂ cup diced carrots

2 cups stewed tomatoes

¹/₂ cup pearl barley

3 whole cloves

Vegetable and Dumpling Soup

3 cups sauerkraut

6 cups mixed vegetables
(cauliflower, peppers,
carrots, parsnip, turnip,
beans, peas, kohlrabi, broad
beans, zucchini, potatoes,
onions, leeks, or celery)

4 qts salted water or stock
salt and pepper to taste

Herb Bouquet No. 6

2 cups sauerkraut juice, or
2-3 Tbsp lemon juice

$^1/_2$ lb lean pork sausage,
cooked and drained

2 eggs

1 $^1/_2$ cups cooked rice

1 tsp dillweed

sour cream

This Romanian soup is made with special dumplings and lots of vegetables. Sour cream gives it both richness and a fine flavor. Serve it with warm wholewheat buns. If sour soup is not to your liking, omit the sauerkraut juice or the lemon.

Chop the sauerkraut and vegetables. Set aside a quart or less of stock to cook dumplings later. In a large pot, boil the sauerkraut and vegetables along with the herb bouquet and pepper in the salted water or stock for about 45-50 minutes. Add the sauerkraut juice or lemon juice.

Coarsely chop the sausages. Mix into dumplings with the eggs, rice, dillweed, salt and pepper. Use wet hands to make small balls. Drop them into hot stock and simmer gently until they are cooked. Add to the soup. Simmer the soup for another few minutes before serving. Stir in the sour cream, or put a spoonful in each plate as you serve the soup.

Brown Sauerkraut Soup

10-12 servings

One day when I was hard put to think of what would feed a bunch of hungry kids, not to mention a hard-working husband, I began to put things into a pot and came up with this recipe. We enjoyed it enough so that it became part of my "make it again" recipes.

Into a large soup pot, put the water, meat, bay leaves, and cloves. Bring to a boil, skim if needed, reduce heat, then simmer until meat is well done. Remove meat from stock. Add sauerkraut, rice, carrots, and cook slowly for about 35-45 minutes or until the vegetables are almost tender. Add the potatoes and mushrooms and cook for another 20 minutes or so.

In a small skillet, fry the onions in oil until translucent. Add the flour, and stir until it is browned. Add some soup stock, stirring rapidly to make a smooth paste, adding more stock as needed. Stir the browned flour and onion into the soup. It should be a nice brown color. Add parsley, dill, and season to taste. The meat could be reserved to serve as a separate dish, or chopped and returned to the soup.

The Egg Drop Dumplings are added at the very last. They are dropped into the soup and cook in 3-5 minutes.

10 cups water

4 or more pork hocks, or
3 lbs lean spare ribs

3-4 bay leaves

4-5 whole cloves

4 cups sauerkraut

1/2 cup washed rice

1 cup carrots, diced

2 potatoes in 1-inch dice

1 cup mushroom slices, or
1 can of sliced mushrooms
with liquid

1 large onion, chopped

3 Tbsp cooking oil

3-4 Tbsp all-purpose flour

1 Tbsp parsley

1 tbsp fresh dill, chopped

salt and pepper to taste

Egg Drop Dumplings
(see index)

Thick Cabbage Soup

4 lbs short ribs

1 meaty shinbone

1 1/2 lbs marrow bones

2 large carrots

1 large parsnip

9 cups water

3 Tbsp tomato paste or 10-oz can stewed tomatoes

1 Herb Bouquet No. 2 (see index)

salt and pepper to taste

Some families like just a hint of tartness to their soup. This Russian-style soup is thick with cabbage and other vegetables, but to get the richness, you must first make the broth or soup stock. It takes a few hours to make; however, the slow cooking develops the flavor and the soup is a meal in itself. Serve it with any black bread—dark rye, light rye, with or without caraway—or pumpernickel.

The Soup Stock

Preheat oven to 500° F.

Place the ribs, shinbone, and marrow bones in a large baking pan. Cut the vegetables into quarters and add to the pan. Brown these ingredients in the hot oven for about 20 minutes, turning occasionally to brown evenly. Remove the baking pan from the oven, and put the browned bones into a large stock pot.

Remove the grease from the baking pan; pour 3 cups water into the pan and cook, stirring, over high heat until all the brown bits are loosened. Add this broth to the stock pot with 9 cups of water, tomato, herb bouquet, salt—about 1 Tbsp — and pepper to taste. Bring the broth to a boil, skim, reduce heat, and simmer, partially covered, for 2 to 2 1/2 hours. Discard the vegetables and the bones. Chill the stock so the grease can be removed easily.

The Soup

Shred the cabbage to obtain approximately 14 cups.

Melt the oil and butter into a large pan and sauté the chopped onion, celery, carrots, and leeks over medium-low heat for about 10-15 minutes until they begin to wilt. Add the shredded cabbage and the sauerkraut; cook over low heat until wilted, another 5 minutes or so. Add 1 cup of liquid from stock pot, cover pan and simmer for 30-40 minutes, adding more stock if necessary.

Add the cabbage mixture to the degreased soup stock. Add the diced tomatoes, lemon juice, and sugar. Simmer for another 30 minutes. Check the seasoning. Serve with a couple of spoonfuls of sour cream and sprinkle with fresh dill or dried dillweed.

3 lbs green cabbage

3 Tbsp cooking oil

3 Tbsp butter

1 cup chopped onion

1 cup chopped celery

1 cup chopped carrots

3 leeks, white part only

stock

3 cups drained sauerkraut

2 cups diced tomatoes

3 Tbsp lemon juice

3 Tbsp sugar

2 cups sour cream

salt and pepper to taste

¹/₂ cup chopped fresh dill or 1 Tbsp dried dillweed

Anything Goes Soup

2 lbs pork shanks, ham hocks, or pig's feet

2 qts cold water

1 medium onion, peeled

3 bay leaves

5-7 whole peppercorns

3 sprigs fresh parsley

2 cups meat broth, bouillon, or meat stock

3 cups sauerkraut

2 cups shredded cabbage

1/3 cup raisins

1 apple, diced

salt and pepper to taste

4-6 slices bacon, fried crisp, drained, and diced

1/2 cup or more chopped green onion

3 Tbsp cooking oil

2 Tbsp flour

potato dumplings (see index)

1/2 cup chopped meat (from pork bones, leftover chicken, wieners, or ham)

This soup can be added to or changed in any way you like. It is a pork-based soup, but, one day I couldn't find any pork in the freezer, so I used a chicken. The resulting soup was nice. I have added or deleted vegetables. Once, I forgot to thicken the soup with flour, but it was good anyway. I have sometimes used raisins and apple to sweeten the dish if the sauerkraut was strong. If your stock is meatless, add leftover meat at the end. This is a thick, hearty soup, a meal in itself.

Put the pork shanks or any other meat bones into a large kettle. Cover with the cold water, bring to a boil, reduce heat, and simmer for about 20 minutes, skimming as needed. Add the whole onion, bay leaves, peppercorns, and the parsley. Cook for about 45 minutes until the meat is tender. Remove the meat, then strain the resulting liquid.

Put the broth, bouillon or meat stock, and the liquid from the bones into the large kettle. Add the sauerkraut, the green cabbage, raisins, and apple, and simmer for an hour. Add salt and pepper, the diced bacon and the green onion. Simmer for another 30 minutes. Mix the oil, flour and 2 Tbsp of water into a smooth paste; stir into the soup.

Make the potato dumplings, and add to the simmering soup. Cook covered for 2-3 minutes. Meanwhile, remove the meat from the bones and cube, discarding skin and gristle; or cut leftover roast or other meat into 1/2-inch cubes and add to the soup. Correct seasonings and serve.

Hot Spicy Soup

For those who enjoy nip to their soup, here is a combination of tart and hot flavors. It is an excellent soup for any day, but it is especially good on a very cold one or after skiing.

In a large, deep pot melt the butter, adding the oil. Brown the meats on all sides, turning as needed. Remove the meat and set aside. Add onions to the pan and cook until transparent. Add wine and stir until all the brown bits are incorporated into the liquid. Stir in the broth, sauerkraut, anise seed, parsley, celery, Tabasco sauce, chili peppers, and cayenne. If you find the soup too spicy, omit the cayenne and some of the hot peppers. Bring to a boil, reduce heat, then simmer, covered, for about 2 hours until the flavors are well-blended and the ingredients are tender. Remove the ham hock, cool slightly, remove the fat, bones, and skin. Shred the meat. Chop the sausages into bite-size pieces. Skim accumulated fat from soup. Return the meats to the soup. Correct the seasonings. Serve with a dollop of sour cream in each plate.

3 Tbsp butter

2 Tbsp cooking oil

1 smoked ham hock

1 ½ lbs lean boneless pork

1 lb hot pepperoni sausage, Bavarian smokies, or chorizo

3 onions, chopped

1 cup dry wine

6 cups chicken broth

2 cups sour cream

3 cups fresh or wine cured sauerkraut

1 Tbsp anise seed

¼ cup chopped parsley

½ cup chopped celery

5 drops Tabasco sauce

2-3 finely chopped fresh red chili peppers, or whole dried chili peppers

cayenne pepper to taste

Kapusniaki

Kapusniaki are known throughout the Ukraine, Russia, Poland, and other regions of eastern Europe. The word "kapusta" means cabbage, while "kapusniak" means made of cabbage, and refers to soups in which sour or pickled cabbage is the main ingredient. The tart flavor is enjoyed very much and is characteristic of some of the area's cuisine.

The main ingredient of a *kapusniak* is a pickled cabbage head, sauerkraut, or its juice. Many other ingredients are added to vary these dishes. Very often, a *kapusniak* is thick and is a meal in itself, but if it is to be used as a first course for a special dinner, a lighter soup is served.

Before using a sour cabbage head, squeeze out the juice, chop the cabbage finely, or put it through a grinder. If the cabbage head or sauerkraut is very sour, it can be soaked in cold water before it is used, then drained to remove some of the tartness.

Kapusniak methods of preparation differ with each recipe, and sometimes the region where the recipe originates. In some, the cabbage would be almost cooked before other ingredients are added. In one, which uses mushrooms, the cabbage is well cooked before the mushrooms are blended with it. If you were to use cereals in your recipe, the cabbage would be sautéed first.

Tart Village Soup

4-5 servings

Kvasivka selians'ka

This soup, a change from the heavy consistency of the usual kapusniak, makes thrifty use of the sauerkraut juice that would otherwise be left in the barrel. The soup is light enough to be served as a first course.

In a large saucepan, bring the juice and stock to a boil. Blend together the sour cream, flour, and egg; add a little hot broth to the mixture, stir, and add to saucepan. Simmer for 3 minutes. Add mashed potatoes and sprinkle with dill. Serve with rye bread or croutons.

2 cups sauerkraut juice

2 cups meat stock

1 cup sour cream

2 Tbsp flour

1 large egg

1/2 cup mashed potato

1 tsp chopped fresh dill

rye bread or croutons

Sauerkraut with Buckwheat

5-6 servings

Kapusniak z kashoiu

Cereals are often served with kapusniaki. They are cooked in several ways. In this one, we cook the cereal separately and then combine it with the kapusniak. It is tasty and freezes well.

Heat oil in a heavy pot; cook onions until transparent. Add stock, sauerkraut (squeezed out if a milder taste is preferred), and pepper. Bring to a boil and simmer for 30 minutes. Add buckwheat and more pepper if desired.

1 Tbsp cooking oil

2 large onions, chopped

1 qt lean meat stock

2 cups sauerkraut

1 tsp ground black pepper

2 cups cooked buckwheat (kasha)

6-8 servings

Kapusniak with Cereal

1 ¹/₂ lbs leftover bones

1 carrot, chopped

1 medium onion, chopped

¹/₂ parsnip, chopped

1 parsley root with leaves

6-8 cups water

salt and pepper to taste

4-5 cups sauerkraut

3 ¹/₂ Tbsp butter

1 cup cooked buckwheat (kasha) or other cereal

In this recipe using cereal, a stock is made first; the stock is then ladled over the cooked sauerkraut. Extra zest is added by including some peppercorns.

Combine the first 6 ingredients in a deep stock pot; season. Bring to a rapid boil, and simmer until the stock is well-flavored, approximately 1 ¹/₂ to 2 hours. Remove vegetables.

Meanwhile, squeeze the sauerkraut dry; fry it in 2 ¹/₂ Tbsp butter in a non-stick skillet. Season with ground pepper.

Lightly reheat the buckwheat. Add 1 Tbsp butter.

When serving, put the sauerkraut into bowls and cover with stock. Serve the buckwheat or cereal as a side dish.

Kapusniak a la Zaporozhye

6-8 servings

In the Ukraine, just north of the Black Sea, is Zaporozhye, a historical site on the Dnieper River. There, kapusniak is prepared differently with spices and millet.

Put the meat into a medium-sized pot. Cover with the water, and add garlic, parsley root with leaves, bay leaves, and whole cloves. Bring to a boil, reduce heat, and simmer until the stock is well cooked, 1 ½ to 2 hours. Remove the meat and strain the stock. Add the sauerkraut, and continue simmering until it is partly cooked.

Finely chop the vegetables; sauté in 2 Tbsp butter. Mince the bacon or salt pork; mix with the millet, then add to the vegetables. Sprinkle all with allspice and add to the simmering sauerkraut. Shred the pork.

Serve the kapusniak with a couple of spoonfuls of shredded meat, a spoonful or two of sour cream, and sprinkled with parsley.

1 ½ lbs lean pork

8 cups water

1 clove garlic

1 parsley root with leaves

2 bay leaves

3 whole cloves

5 cups drained sauerkraut

3 large potatoes

1 medium carrot

1 parsnip

1 large onion

3 celery stalks

2 Tbsp butter

2 Tbsp bacon or salt pork

2 Tbsp millet

⅛ tsp allspice

6 Tbsp sour cream

1 tsp minced fresh parsley

Kapusniak with Mushrooms

2 Tbsp dried mushrooms

7-8 cups water

4-5 cups sauerkraut

3 large potatoes, peeled, coarsely chopped

1 large carrot, chopped

3 stalks celery, chopped

1 parsnip, chopped

1 onion, chopped

1-2 cloves garlic, minced

2 Tbsp cooking oil

3 whole peppercorns

2 bay leaves

$^1/_2$ tsp minced fresh parsley

1 tsp minced, fresh dill

Dried mushrooms are often used in the traditional Slavic cuisine. I remember my great-grandmother and my grandmother picking wild mushrooms to be dried for winter use. My mother-in-law also had a good knowledge of edible mushrooms, and drying them was part of her summer chores.

You can substitute fresh mushrooms which do not have to be soaked beforehand. Their flavor is different and not as strong as the dried ones, so adjust your recipe to taste.

Wash the dried mushrooms and soak them until they plump up. Drain. In a large pot, bring the water to a boil, add mushrooms, and simmer for 20-30 minutes. Strain, reserving the liquid. Slice the mushrooms finely.

Put the sauerkraut into the pot, cover with some of the mushroom stock and cook for 20-30 minutes. Cook the potatoes in the remaining mushroom stock. Sauté the rest of the vegetables, and add to pot. Add the sauerkraut together with the bay leaves and peppercorns. Simmer for another 20-30 minutes. Serve the kapusniak sprinkled with the parsley and the dill.

Ordinary Kapusniak

A variety of meats are used in the basic stock for many of the kapusniaki. Beef substitutes for pork or vice versa, but in each case the flavor will be slightly different. Although the following recipe is considered to be a basic kapusniak, it is made flavorful with the addition of bacon, or salt pork, and is further enhanced with a sour cream dressing.

In a medium-sized pot, cover the pork with the water. Add the bay leaves and garlic. Bring to a boil, reduce heat, and simmer until the meat is cooked. Remove the meat and cut it into serving portions. Strain the stock. Add the sauerkraut to the stock, and simmer about 20 minutes, until it is partly cooked.

Sauté the vegetables except for the potatoes along with the parsley root in butter. In a separate pan, brown the flour slightly, stirring constantly to prevent burning; blend the browned flour with the frying vegetables. Cook the bacon lightly, and add it to the sauerkraut with the sautéed vegetables. Bring to a boil and add the diced potatoes. Simmer until the potatoes are cooked.

Serve the kapusniak with portions of the meat on top and a spoonful of the Sour Cream Dressing.

Sour Cream Dressing

Combine the sour cream, the parsley and dill. Grind the peppercorns and stir into the cream.

1 1/2 lb lean pork

8 cups water

2 bay leaves

2 cloves garlic

4-5 cups drained sauerkraut

1-2 carrots, chopped

1 medium onion, minced

1 parsley root with leaves

2 strips bacon, chopped, or

2 Tbsp chopped salt pork

2 Tbsp butter

3 Tbsp flour

3 medium potatoes, diced

salt and pepper to taste

6 Tbsp sour cream

2 Tbsp chopped fresh parsley

2 peppercorns

1 Tbsp chopped fresh dill

Polish Kapusniak

6-8 dried mushrooms

1 ¹/₂ lbs pork meat

1-2 marrow bones

1 onion, baked or fried

1 parsley root with leaves

2 bay leaves

3 whole cloves

6 whole peppercorns

10 cups water

4-5 cups drained sauerkraut

2 carrots, diced

3 stalks celery, diced

1 celery root, diced

1 medium onion, diced

1 parsnip, diced

3 strips bacon or equal amount salt pork, diced

2 Tbsp flour, browned

1 tsp sugar (optional)

3 wieners or equal amount of garlic sausage

salt and pepper to taste

Poland has its own version of kapusniak. The browned flour imparts a nice color to the soup, as well as its own unique flavor. If the soup is too tart, sugar is often used to sweeten it.

Soak the mushrooms in water to cover. In a large pot, place the meat, the bones, the baked and fried onion, the parsley root, bay leaves, whole cloves, the peppercorns, and the 10 cups of water. Bring to a boil, reduce heat, then simmer approximately 1 ¹/₂ hours, until the meat is partially cooked. Skim as necessary. Add the sauerkraut and mushrooms. Continue simmering until the meat is well done, about 2 hours. Remove the meat, debone it, and cut into small pieces.

Remove the mushrooms and cut into strips. Remove the marrow from the bones and add to the soup. Remove the parsley root, the bay leaves, and the whole cloves. Return the meat, mushrooms, and marrow to the pot, sauté the vegetables in butter until lightly browned. Add to the soup.

Brown the diced bacon, then add the browned flour and a small amount of soup stock, stirring to keep the flour from lumping. Add small amounts of soup stock until the flour and liquid form a smooth paste. Add the paste to the soup, and bring it to a boil. Season to taste, adding sugar to sweeten the *kapusniak*, if desired.

Just before serving, add the diced wieners or sausage. Serve hot.

Kapusniak

Serve the meat as a separate course. Very good with black or rye bread.

Place the first 6 ingredients in a medium-sized pot. Cover and bring to a boil, reduce heat, and simmer until the meat is tender. Remove the meat and strain the stock.

Add the next 5 ingredients to the stock, and season with salt and pepper. Cook until the vegetables are tender. Remove the vegetables from stock, and put through a sieve, or purée them in a blender. Return the meat and the puréed vegetables to the pot.

Add sauerkraut and mushrooms, and cook together gently until the sauerkraut is tender, about 20 minutes.

In a medium-sized skillet, fry the chopped onion in hot fat until it begins to get limp; add the flour and brown with the onion lightly. Add some stock, stirring constantly to prevent lumping. Stir until smooth and return it to the soup. Add the sour cream and correct the seasonings. Add chopped dill, parsley, or both.

2 lbs spare ribs

10 cups water

2 bay leaves

1 clove garlic

3 whole cloves

4-5 whole peppercorns

1 medium onion, chopped

2 medium carrots, diced

2 stalks celery, diced

1 parsnip, diced

2 potatoes, peeled and diced

salt and pepper to taste

4 cups sauerkraut

1 can mushrooms with liquid, or fresh mushrooms, cooked in stock

3 Tbsp chopped onion

2 Tbsp cooking oil

3 Tbsp flour

2 Tbsp sour cream

2 Tbsp chopped parsley and/or dill

Meat Kapusniak

¾ lb boneless pork

3 Tbsp salad oil

1 cup finely chopped onion

2 carrots, diced

1 small parsnip, diced

1 small celery root, diced

3 stalks celery, diced
scrubbed, but unpeeled

4 cups rinsed, drained
sauerkraut

stock or water

½ tsp caraway seed

½ tsp dill seed

2 cloves garlic, minced

½ lb smoked sausage

10-12 small new potatoes,
scrubbed but unpeeled

2-3 Tbsp flour

1 cup diced bacon

Kapusniak z miasom

Inspired by Ukrainian cuisine, this meat kapusniak makes use of a variety of vegetables, including celery root. Small new potatoes are cooked whole and served with each bowl of soup. It looks good and tastes even better!

Cut the pork into 1-inch cubes. Heat 1 Tbsp salad oil in a Dutch oven, and brown the meat, turning it often. Add ½ cup chopped onion along with the carrots, parsnip, celery root, and celery. Cover, and cook over very low heat for 1 hour or until meat is almost tender.

Chop the sauerkraut. Add to the meat and vegetables and cover with stock or water. Add caraway and dill seeds, and minced garlic. Cut the sausage into bite-size pieces and add it too. Brown flour lightly in 2 Tbsp oil. Add sufficient stock to make a smooth paste before adding to the soup.

Cook potatoes in salted water until tender; drain and leave on low heat for 1 minute to dry.

Fry the bacon in a non-stick skillet until partly cooked; then add ½ cup finely chopped onion and sauté until transparent. Sprinkle over the potatoes to distribute evenly. Put in 1-2 potatoes in each serving bowl and serve the soup over them.

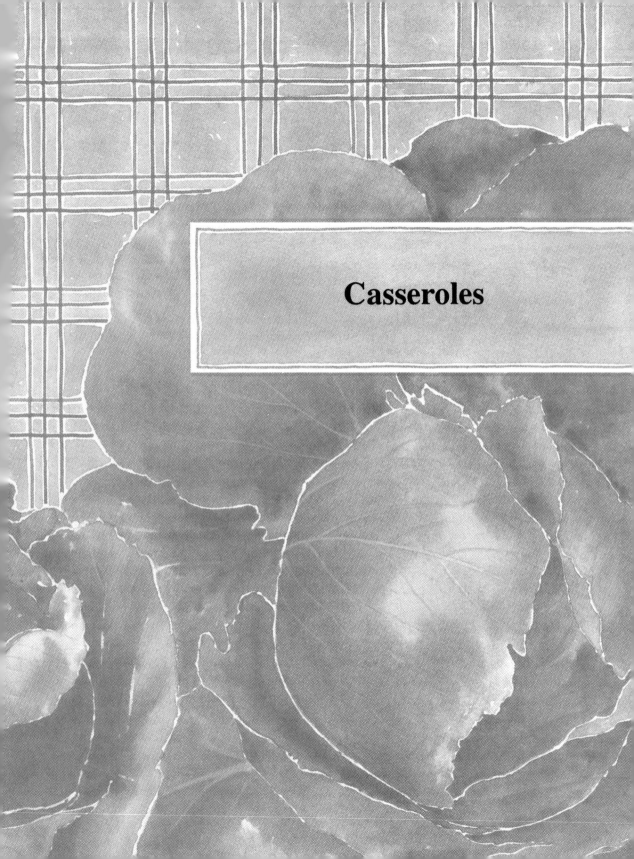

Casseroles

Casseroles

Casseroles are a boon to busy cooks. They can be served as a one-pot meal or as a side dish. Ingredients may include fresh or cooked vegetables, leftovers, or any meat insufficient for another meal. You can combine such ingredients with rice, pot barley, or pasta. Mushrooms of any kind are excellent additions and will make an ordinary dish into a gourmet meal.

In my youth, I believed that all the special dishes my mother cooked were uniquely Ukrainian, but I came to realize that other Slavic countries had similar recipes. Wherever they originated, all are good to eat.

Sauerkraut and Pea Casserole

4-6 servings

1 cup dried peas or 19-oz can chick peas

2 tbsp dried mushrooms

4 cups sauerkraut

1 onion, chopped

1-2 cloves garlic, minced (optional)

1 cup sour cream

salt and pepper to taste

Peas and mushrooms with the sauerkraut make this casserole doubly delicious.

Soak the peas overnight, then cover in 3 cups cold, lightly salted water and bring to the boil for 1 minute. Reduce heat and simmer until tender. Drain and set aside.

Soak the dried mushrooms in a small amount of water. Simmer in the same water until they are plump and tender. Drain, reserving the liquid. Chop and set aside.

Put the sauerkraut, the mushroom liquid, chopped mushrooms, onion, garlic, sour cream in a medium-sized pot; season with salt and pepper. Simmer for an hour or more.

Preheat oven to 350° F.

In an ovenproof casserole dish, put one-third of the sauerkraut, followed by one-third of the peas. Repeat the layers together with their liquid, which should reach almost to the top of the casserole. Make up any deficiency in the liquid with water. Bake for approximately 30-45 minutes.

Peas and Sauerkraut

4-6 servings

The dish Sryata Vechera—Peas and Sauerkraut—is the lenten-style dish served for supper on the Ukrainian Christmas Eve. On this occasion, meats and animal fats—including cream—are omitted from the dish's preparation, although the casserole is served at other times when bacon and cream may be used. At Christmas, the dish is brought to the table when the first star appears in the eastern sky. This meal is limited to family members, and it is followed by a trip to the church for a special Christmas service.

Simmer the sauerkraut in boiling water for 20-30 minutes.

Preheat oven to 350° F.

In a large skillet, fry the bacon or salt pork until almost crisp. Remove with a slotted spoon and set aside. Use the bacon fat to fry the onion lightly. Add the flour and cook, stirring frequently until the flour begins to brown. Add a little oil if there is not enough bacon fat. Add some stock from the sauerkraut to make a smooth gravy.

Stir the gravy into the sauerkraut. Add the cooked peas, mushrooms, garlic, peppercorns, and bacon. Stir in the sour cream, and correct the seasonings. Put into a casserole and bake for 30-45 minutes.

4 cups rinsed, drained sauerkraut

1 cup boiling water

²/₃ cup salt pork or bacon, diced

1 medium onion, chopped

3 Tbsp flour

stock

1 cup cooked dried peas

²/₃ cups cooked, sliced mushrooms

2 cloves garlic, crushed

4 peppercorns

3 Tbsp sour cream

salt and pepper to taste

Tomato Scallops with Sauerkraut

6 servings

3-4 Tbsp butter

1 medium onion, minced

3 cups rinsed, drained sauerkraut

3 cups stewed tomatoes or a 28-oz can stewed tomatoes

1/2 tsp dried basil

salt to taste

pepper to taste

1/2 cup bread crumbs

A quick supper dish is made with tomatoes and sauerkraut. Put the casserole in the oven first, and by the time the potatoes are cooked and mashed, and the meat is sliced, all is ready to serve.

Preheat oven to 350° F.

Sauté the onion in 1 Tbsp butter in a medium-sized pan. Add the sauerkraut. Mix well.

Drain the tomatoes, reserving the liquid. Chop the tomatoes and place in a greased casserole dish. Season the tomatoes with basil, salt if the sauerkraut is not salty, and pepper. Dot with butter and add a layer of crumbs. Follow with a layer of onion-sauerkraut. Repeat layers until all the ingredients are used, reserving some crumbs for the last layer. Add the tomato liquid. Bake for 30-35 minutes.

Sauerkraut and Tomato Casserole

8-10 servings

4 cups stewed tomatoes

5 cups drained sauerkraut

pepper

1/4 cup brown sugar

1/2 cup diced bacon

1 large onion, chopped

The addition of one or two different ingredients results in a casserole with a different texture and flavor.

Preheat oven to 350° F.

Purée the tomatoes. Combine the sauerkraut, tomatoes, pepper, and brown sugar in a medium-sized pot.

Sauté the bacon and onion in oil in a non-stick skillet until golden. Add half to the sauerkraut mixture and reserve half for garnish.

Put the sauerkraut mixture into a buttered casserole, and bake for 50-60 minutes, uncovering for the last 20 minutes to brown lightly. Sprinkle with bacon and onion on top before serving.

Rice with Bacon Casserole

4-6 servings

Rice is an excellent ingredient to use in one-dish meals. This one also incorporates leeks and celery along with sauerkraut to make a filling, tasty meal, or, if you are extra hungry, make a side dish.

Preheat oven to 350° F.

In a non-stick skillet, fry the leeks and celery with the bacon until they are limp. Butter a 3-4 qt casserole; add half the sauerkraut, one-third of the fried bacon, leeks, and celery, and half the washed rice. Repeat layers once more ending with rice. Top with the remaining leek-celery-bacon mixture. Season to taste. Add enough water or stock to cover the rice.

Bake for about an hour and 15 minutes, or until the rice is cooked. Add a bit more liquid during the cooking, if necessary.

2 large leeks, thinly sliced

1/2 cup celery, sliced

1/2 lb bacon, diced

butter or margarine

4 cups drained, rinsed, sauerkraut

1 1/4 cup washed rice

salt and pepper to taste

chicken stock, tomato juice, or boiling water

Apple Ring Sauerkraut

4-6 servings

Apples are often used with sauerkraut. They impart a delicate flavor and sweetness. This dish is decorated with apple slices.

Preheat oven broiler.

In a medium-sized saucepan, mix the onion, vinegar, caraway seeds, the salt and pepper with the sauerkraut and its juice. Stir well. Simmer over low heat for about 30 minutes. Place the apple slices on top of the sauerkraut mixture and continue simmering until the apple slices are almost soft. Lift them off and set aside.

Put the sauerkraut into a shallow baking dish; arrange the apple slices in rows across the top. Sprinkle with sugar and broil.

1 onion, chopped

1 Tbsp vinegar

1 tsp caraway seeds (optional)

salt and pepper to taste

4 cups undrained sauerkraut

4 apples, peeled, cored, cut in 1/4-inch slices

sugar to taste

Baked Sauerkraut

1 onion, chopped

1/4 cup diced bacon

3 cups drained sauerkraut

3 apples, cored, sliced

1-2 Tbsp prepared mustard

salt and pepper to taste

1/2 cup water

1-2 Tbsp molasses

1 tsp dry mustard

Here's another apple-sauerkraut combination with a unique flavor. Molasses and mustard transform an otherwise ordinary dish into something delectably delicious.

Preheat oven to 350° F.

In a non-stick skillet, fry the onion and bacon until wilted. Add the sauerkraut, apple slices, prepared mustard, salt and pepper; add the water, and simmer gently for about 15 minutes.

Butter a 2-qt casserole dish and put in the prepared sauerkraut. Top with molasses and dry mustard. Bake for about 30-35 minutes. Serve hot.

6 servings

Simple Baked Sauerkraut

3/4 lb pork shanks or hocks

6-8 cups water

1 large onion, chopped

1 tsp salt

3 bay leaves

4 whole cloves

4 cups sauerkraut

Adding meat to a casserole can create a one-dish supper or lunch. The long, slow cooking allows you to use many of the cheaper cuts of meat without losing flavor or tenderness. This simple dish uses pork shanks or pork hocks and may be served with dumplings if you wish.

In a large saucepan, cover the meat with water and bring to a boil. Simmer for about 20 minutes, skimming surface as needed. Add the onion, salt, bay leaves, and the whole cloves. Simmer for 2-3 hours, until the meat is tender. Remove the meat and strain the stock if necessary.

Preheat oven to 350° F.

Put the sauerkraut in a baking pan and arrange the meat on top. Add one cup of the pork stock, or more as needed. Bake for 30-40 minutes. Serve hot.

Goulash from Szekely

In Hungary, in the Szekely area, there are several ways of making goulash, a kind of stew. The following two recipes are cooked casserole style. Both have enough meat to use as a main dish. Serve with creamed mashed potatoes, fresh peas, and a salad.

Preheat oven to 350° F.

Brown the meat in the oil in a large non-stick skillet. Put the meat and the sauerkraut in a deep casserole dish. Add the tomatoes and onion to the sauerkraut; stir in the seasonings. Cover and bake for 1 ½ hours, or until the meat is cooked and tender. Add a little more water if more liquid is needed during cooking. Stir in the sour cream before serving.

1 ½ lb lean veal or beef, cubed

1 ½ lbs lean stewing pork, cubed

3 Tbsp oil

4 cups rinsed, drained sauerkraut

1 ½ cups crushed, or chopped, stewed tomatoes

1 onion, chopped

1 tsp dried basil

1 ½ tsp caraway seeds

salt and pepper to taste

2 cups sour cream

Goulash, Szekely Style

3 cups drained sauerkraut

2 Tbsp cooking oil

1 ¹/₂ lbs lean pork, cubed

¹/₂ cup chopped chives

2 cloves garlic, minced

1 ¹/₂ tsp paprika

salt and pepper to taste

¹/₂ cup sour cream

sour cream to garnish
(optional)

For the authentic flavor, use Hungarian paprika in this dish.

Preheat oven to 350° F.

Fry the sauerkraut lightly in oil in a non-stick skillet, and put into a buttered casserole. Brown the meat slightly; add chives, and fry for another minute or two. Remove from heat and add the minced garlic, paprika, salt and pepper to taste. Add to the casserole and stir lightly to mix with the sauerkraut.

Bake until pork is tender, 1 ¹/₂ hours. Let the ingredients cool slightly, then add the sour cream. Stir well to mix. Serve hot with a spoonful of sour cream, if desired.

Paprika Surprise

2 large onions, diced

1 Tbsp cooking oil

2 Tbsp flour

2 cups water

¹/₂ cup diced celery

¹/₂ cup diced green peppers

10 ¹/₂-oz can condensed tomato soup

1-2 Tbsp paprika

2 Tbsp sugar

2 ¹/₂-3 cups sauerkraut

Paprika is a favorite ingredient in Hungarian cuisine. This is an excellent side dish.

In a large non-stick skillet, brown the onions in oil. Sprinkle with flour and stir until well blended and smooth. Add the water slowly, stirring constantly. In a bowl, combine the remaining ingredients; add to the skillet, and simmer slowly for about 1 ¹/₂ hours.

Hungarian Rice and Sauerkraut

8-10 servings

Another dish inspired by Hungarian cookery is this rice dish which makes use of spicy sausages and garlic. Use lots of onions with this one.

Parboil rice with ¹/₂ cup chopped onions about 8-10 minutes.

In a separate pot, cook the sauerkraut with the bacon rind over moderate heat for 25-30 minutes. Discard the bacon rind.

In a medium-sized non-stick skillet, fry the pork pieces with the remaining onions in bacon fat. Add the garlic, seasonings, cayenne, the sausage, and bacon.

Preheat oven to 350° F.

Butter or grease a large baking dish. Put in layers of sauerkraut, rice, and meat, repeating the layers, ending with sauerkraut. Cover with sour cream, coaxing it to dribble down the layers.

Cover the casserole and bake for about 1 hour, or until the meat is tender, and the rice is fluffy.

1 cup washed rice

5-6 onions chopped

6 cups sauerkraut

bacon rind

2 lbs pork, chopped

5-6 Tbsp bacon fat

3 cloves garlic, crushed

¹/₄ tsp cayenne

salt, pepper, and paprika to taste

1 lb spicy, fat sausage, sliced

¹/₂ lb bacon, cubed

2 cups sour cream

Corned Beef and Sauerkraut

6 servings

Corned beef goes so well with sauerkraut that even a casserole is created with it. This zesty combination is given an extra tang with horseradish and mustard.

Preheat oven to 400° F.

Grease a 2-qt baking dish, and put the sauerkraut on the bottom.

In a large bowl, combine the mashed corned beef, tomato juice, onion, garlic, horseradish, and mustard. Mix well and spread over the sauerkraut. Cut the bacon into 1-inch strips and place over the top.

Bake for 25-30 minutes.

3-4 cups drained sauerkraut

1 large or 2 small cans corned beef, mashed

1 or more cups tomato juice

¹/₂ to 1 cup chopped onion

2 cloves garlic, minced

2 tsp prepared horseradish

1 tsp dry mustard

2 strips bacon

Sauerkraut with Navy Beans

1 ¹/₂ cups dried white beans

³/₄ cup diced bacon

1 onion, diced

3 cloves garlic, minced

4 cups rinsed, drained, sauerkraut

3 carrots cut into ¹/₄-inch slices

3 stalks celery cut into diagonal pieces

1 large apple, cored, diced

2 or more cups apple juice

3-4 bay leaves

4-5 whole cloves

pepper to taste

2 lbs assorted smoked meats cut in bite-size pieces

This recipe is reminscent of the French Choucroute, but with the addition of navy beans becomes a different dish. It is excellent warmed up the next day, too.

Preheat oven to 300° F.

Soak the beans overnight. Pour off the water and fill the pot with fresh cold water. Put on to simmer until the beans are tender. Drain, set aside.

In a non-stick skillet, fry the bacon until it is translucent; add the onion and garlic and sauté until soft. Put them into a Dutch oven; add sauerkraut, the carrots, celery, apple, apple juice, bay leaves, cloves, and pepper to taste.

Bake in the oven for 2 ¹/₂ to 3 hours; add the sausages and the cooked, drained beans. Mix to blend and bake for another 20-30 minutes.

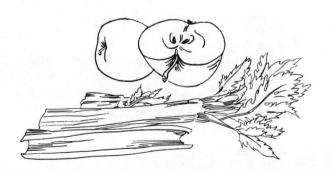

Lima Bean Casserole

4 servings

Add some green peppers, some sausage meat, a few spices, and tomato juice to lima beans or broad beans to make a satisfying dish.

Preheat oven to 350° F.

Simmer the lima beans in water until almost tender. Drain.

Add the celery seeds, brown sugar, and savory to the tomato juice. Season with salt and pepper.

In a large skillet, fry the sausage meat; remove from heat, drain off the fat, and break up the meat with a fork. Add the onion, celery, green peppers, the cooked lima beans, and the tomato juice mixture.

Grease a shallow baking dish. Put in a layer of sauerkraut; then a layer of lima bean-sausage mixture. Repeat layers, ending with the lima bean-sausage mixture. Top with bread crumbs. Bake for 30-40 minutes.

3/4 lb dried lima beans

1/2 tsp celery seeds

2 Tbsp brown sugar

1/2 tsp savory

1 1/2 cups tomato juice

salt and pepper to taste

1 1/2 lbs pork sausage meat

1 onion chopped

1/2 cup chopped celery

3/4 cup chopped green peppers

3 cups drained sauerkraut

soft bread crumbs

Ribs and Kraut

6 servings

This method of cooking spare ribs makes a satisfying meal, and while the recipe takes long, slow cooking, there is little work involved. Supper can be baking while you do something else.

Preheat oven to 325° F.

In a large casserole or roasting pan, place the ingredients in layers, starting with sauerkraut. Sprinkle with chopped onions, pour in tomato sauce, add the cubed potatoes, sprinkle with sugar, and place the ribs last. Do not stir. Cover and bake for about 3 hours until the meat is well cooked.

Variation: Add Spaetzle (see index) or Egg Drop Dumplings (see index) before serving.

3 cups drained sauerkraut

1 cup onion, chopped

1 1/2 10-oz cans tomato sauce

2 large potatoes, cubed

1/4 cup firm packed brown sugar

3 lbs spare ribs cut in serving pieces

Pork with Sauerkraut

1 ¹/₂ lbs lean pork, cubed

¹/₃ cup drippings

³/₄ cup chopped onions

2 cloves garlic, minced

¹/₂ tsp caraway seeds (optional)

1-2 small hot peppers, chopped

2 Tbsp tomato paste

4 cups drained sauerkraut

1 cup or more beef or chicken bouillon

1 tsp paprika

Pork is the favored meat with sauerkraut. The tartness of the sauerkraut enhances the sweetness of the pork. Bulgarians marry the two ingredients in this casserole.

Preheat oven to 350-375° F.

In a large ovenproof casserole or skillet, fry the cubed meat in the drippings. Remove the meat from the pan; using the same drippings, fry the onions, garlic, caraway, and chopped peppers, until the onion is translucent. Add the tomato paste, thinned with a little hot water. Mix in the sauerkraut. Cook for a few minutes until the sauerkraut is limp. Add the meat and pour half the bouillon over the top, adding more if needed. Sprinkle with the paprika. Simmer gently until the meat is almost cooked, 50-60 minutes.

Place the casserole or skillet in the oven for another 30 minutes or more, adding more liquid if necessary. Do not make the dish too soupy; it should be very thick.

6 servings

Apple Pork Chops

6 thick pork chops

3 cups drained sauerkraut

2 apples, cored, chopped

4 Tbsp catsup

4 Tbsp water

1 ¹/₂ Tbsp corn syrup

¹/₂ tsp pepper

1 tsp salt

1 tsp dry mustard

1 level tsp barbecue seasoning

Pork chops, cooked with apples and sauerkraut, and a barbecue spice have an extra savor.

Preheat oven to 350° F.

Trim fat from the pork chops. In a large, non-stick skillet, fry them slowly until the chops are browned on both sides. Put the drained sauerkraut into a casserole, add chopped apples, and stir well. Place pork chops on top.

In the skillet stir together the catsup, water, and corn syrup, along with the spices. Heat slowly, stirring constantly, until boiling. Pour over the chops. Cover the casserole tightly and bake for 30-40 minutes; uncover and bake for another 30 minutes until the meat is tender.

East-West Casserole

Pork chops are the principal ingredient in this casserole, but a little wine and some vegetables give their own unique piquancy. This dish comes from Germany.

Preheat oven to 375° F.

Season the pork chops with garlic salt and pepper. Heat the oil or butter in a non-stick skillet and brown the pork chops on both sides. Remove the chops and add the onions and apples, cooking slowly until they begin to color. Remove from the pan. Sauté the sauerkraut in the remaining fat, adding more if necessary.

In an ovenproof casserole, layer sauerkraut with onion-apple mixture, all carrots and potatoes, then another layer of sauerkraut, onions, etc., and place the chops on top. Add the hot stock and white wine. Cover and bake about an hour or until tender.

6 pork chops, 1-inch thick

garlic salt

pepper to taste

2 Tbsp oil or butter

2 medium onions, diced

2-3 apples, peeled, cored, diced

4 cups drained sauerkraut

2 carrots, sliced $^1/_8$-inch thick

1 $^1/_2$ lbs potatoes, peeled, and sliced $^1/_2$-inch thick

1 $^1/_2$ cups hot meat stock

$^1/_2$ cup white wine

Country-Style Ribs

6 servings

Some people like very simple dishes that take only a few minutes to prepare. Here is another way to prepare tasty ribs.

Preheat oven to 300°-325° F.

Mix the sauerkraut and sugar in a large baking pan. Peel the potatoes, leave them whole, and place on top of the sauerkraut. Cut the ribs into serving portions and place on top of the potatoes. Season with salt and pepper to taste.

Bake for about 3 hours, turning the ribs once or twice to brown on both sides. Serve on a platter with the ribs on the outside. Place the sauerkraut in the middle and circle with the potatoes.

3 cups sauerkraut

$^1/_4$ cup firmly packed brown sugar

6 small or medium potatoes

4-5 lbs spare ribs

salt and pepper

Hearty Sauerkraut Supper

6 pork ribs

2 Tbsp cooking oil

3 celery stalks, cut in larger pieces

1 onion, diced

1 ³/₄ cups apple juice

4 cups sauerkraut

1 lb squash cut in 1 ¹/₂-inch cubes

2 red apples, cut in ¹/₂-inch slices

3 medium potatoes cut in ¹/₂-inch slices

salt and pepper to taste

No stock on hand? This cook decided to use apple juice, with excellent results.

Preheat oven to 350° F; preheat a large non-stick skillet.

In the preheated skillet, brown the ribs in oil. Remove. Fry the celery and onions in the skillet, stirring, until they begin to color. Remove from pan. Add the apple juice to the skillet, stirring to loosen the brown bits in the pan.

In a 13-inch by 9-inch baking pan, combine the sauerkraut with the celery and onion. Top with squash, apples, and potato slices. Pour the apple juice over it. Tuck the ribs into the sauerkraut mixture, season with salt and pepper to taste.

Cover tightly and bake for about 2 hours or until tender.

Pork Chop Bake

2 cups sauerkraut

1 onion, chopped

2 cloves garlic, minced

4 thick pork chops

1 tsp pepper

Another simply made dish.

Preheat oven to 350° F.

Mix the sauerkraut, onion, and garlic in the bottom of a casserole. Season the chops with pepper and place them on top. Cover and bake for an hour or more, until the chops are tender. Uncover, and bake for another 20 minutes or so to let them brown.

Bavarian Pork Hocks

4 servings

Pork hocks, smoked or otherwise, are a cheap cut of meat, but slow cooking and added ingredients make for a flavorful dish.

Using a large Dutch oven, put the hocks into cold water, together with pepper, salt, bay leaves, whole cloves, garlic, onion, and celery leaves. Bring to a boil and skim. Reduce heat and simmer until tender, about 3 hours. Drain.

Preheat oven to 325° F.

Place the hocks in a casserole. Top with sauerkraut, the brown sugar, and apple wedges. Cover, and bake for about an hour.

4 pork hocks, ³/₄ lbs each

2 cups cold water

salt and pepper to taste

2 bay leaves

3 whole cloves

1 clove garlic, minced

1 onion, sliced

¹/₂ cup finely chopped celery leaves

3 cups sauerkraut

¹/₄ cup packed brown sugar

a tart apple, cut into 8 wedges

German-Style Pigs' Knuckles

6 pigs' knuckles, scraped
and scrubbed

1-2 Tbsp butter

1 large onion, diced

2 cloves garlic

5 cups drained sauerkraut

salt and pepper to taste

3 bay leaves

3-4 whole cloves

1 tsp caraway seeds

dry white wine or water

Pigs knuckles are usually thought of as being good only for soup. Here, in this casserole, they give flavor to what would otherwise be a very ordinary dish.

Preheat oven to 325° F.

In a large Dutch oven, heat the butter, adding the onion, the whole garlic cloves, and cook until lightly browned. Add the sauerkraut and seasonings. Stir and cook for 5-6 minutes. Add the pigs' knuckles, pushing them down into the sauerkraut. Add enough wine or water just to reach the level of the sauerkraut. Cover, and bring to a boil. Place in the oven to simmer slowly for 3-4 hours. The meat should be very tender.

Variations:
- Add potatoes or dumplings to make a one-dish supper.
- Use ham hocks to make the dish Polish style.

Roast Pork with Sauerkraut

5-6 lbs pork roast

3-4 garlic cloves, coarsely
chopped

4 cups drained sauerkraut

1/2 tsp caraway seeds

10-oz can tomato sauce with
mushrooms

1 envelope onion soup

You can dress up pork roasts with sauerkraut and other goodies. A surprise ingredient is onion soup.

Preheat oven to 300-325° F.

In an open roasting pan, bake the meat and garlic for about 3 hours. When nearly cooked, remove the roast from the pan and place it on a plate in a warm place.

To the drippings in the roasting pan, add the sauerkraut, caraway, the tomato sauce, the onion soup mix, reserving 2 tsp, and stir well. Return meat to the pan. Mix the remaining onion soup mix with a little water and glaze the roast with the mixture. Return the roasting pan and its contents to the oven and continue cooking for another 30-40 minutes or until the meat is completely tender.

Stuffed Roast Pork

8-10 servings

A Bavarian specialty!

Preheat oven to 325° F.

Place the meat on a board with the rib ends up and the meat side towards you. Cut each chop down to the bone to make a pocket for the stuffing, or have the butcher do this. Mix the remaining ingredients, except the gravy and the potatoes, to make the filling. Mix well, and stuff about a half cup or so into each pocket. Tie the roast with a string and place in a roasting pan.

Roast, allowing 30-35 minutes per pound, or about 3 hours. After 2 hours, add the potatoes. Add water to the pan if necessary and cover the pan for the last hour or so.

To serve, remove the roast to heated platter, cut the string, and divide into chops. Surround roast with potatoes. Serve with Brown Pork Gravy.

6 lbs loin of pork

1 large apple, diced

2 cups (4 slices) half-dried bread crumbs

1/2 cup diced celery

1 tsp chopped dill

3 cloves garlic, minced

1 medium onion, minced

1 tsp poultry seasoning

1/2 cup seedless raisins

salt and pepper to taste

3 cups drained, chopped sauerkraut

12 medium potatoes, peeled

Brown Pork Gravy

After the meat has been removed from the pan, pour off the fat. Add 1/2 cup water and Worcestershire sauce to taste; stir, scraping off all the brown bits until liquid boils. Take the flour, and add sufficient cold water or stock to make a thin paste. Add to the boiling liquid in the pan, and stir vigorously until the gravy thickens and begins to bubble. Slowly add water to make 2 cups of gravy, stirring to avoid lumps. Boil at least 1 minute. Season with salt and pepper to taste, and a few drops of gravy browning for color.

Worcestershire sauce to taste

1/2 cup water

4 Tbsp flour

gravy browning

Ukrainian Spareribs

3 lbs or more spareribs, cut
in serving-size pieces

3/4 tsp salt

1 cup boiling water

1 onion, diced

3 bay leaves

3 whole cloves

4 cups drained sauerkraut

2 tsp sugar

salt and pepper to taste

*2 cups beef or chicken stock,
or consommé*

*Egg Drop Dumplings
(see index)*

*This is my favorite way to have spareribs if I am not
having them barbecued.*

Brown the ribs in a skillet; then put them into a Dutch
oven. Add the salt and water, onion, bay leaves, and
whole cloves. Simmer until tender, about 1 to 1 1/2 hours.
Add the sauerkraut and sugar. Season to taste, and cook
for another 30 minutes or so, until the flavors blend.

In saucepan, bring the soup stock to a boil and drop
into it some Egg Drop Dumplings. Cover and cook until
they are fluffy. Drain and add the dumplings to the
sauerkraut and ribs just before serving.

Pork Back Ribs

3 lbs pork loin or back ribs

1 tsp salad oil

12-oz can beer

1 tsp salt

4 cups sauerkraut

1 cup diced onion

2 Tbsp brown sugar

*Beer is used as the liquid in this dish of Pork Back Ribs.
Brown sugar is added for sweetness and sauerkraut for
tartness.*

Cut the ribs into serving portions, and brown them in
the oil in a large skillet. Turn the ribs into a Dutch
oven. Add the beer and the salt. Bring to a boil, reduce the heat,
and simmer for 35-40 minutes. Stir in the sauerkraut, the
onion, and the brown sugar; cover and continue cooking
over low heat for another 45 minutes to 1 hour, until the
meat is tender.

May be served with Liver Dumplings (see index).

Sauerkraut Supper

One-pot suppers not only save time and fuel—they are very tasty!

Preheat oven to 350° F.

In a large skillet, brown the pork chops in the salad oil. Remove the chops, and cook the onion and green pepper in the drippings until softened. Add some apple juice, and stir to loosen the brown bits left by the pork chops.

Put the sauerkraut into a Dutch oven. Add the onion mixture and stir well. Add the carrots, celery root, potatoes, and apple slices. Pour in the apple juice and mix in the brown sugar. Season with salt and pepper to taste. Tuck the pork chops among the vegetables.

Cover tightly and bake for 2 hours, or longer, basting occasionally with apple juice, until the meat and vegetables are tender.

6 pork ribs or loin chops, each $^3/_4$ inch thick

2 tbsp salad oil

1 onion, diced

$^1/_2$ cup diced green pepper

1 $^3/_4$ cups apple juice

4 cups sauerkraut

3 carrots, julienned

1 cup celery root, diced

4-5 medium potatoes, cut in large pieces

2 apples, cored, cut in $^1/_2$-inch pieces

2 Tbsp brown sugar

salt and pepper to taste

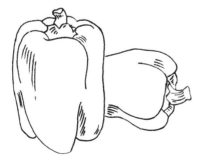

Casseroles   93

Pork Shoulder in Cream Sauce

4 cups sauerkraut

2 onions, chopped

3 Tbsp cooking oil

3 Tbsp flour

1 tsp paprika

1 tsp sage

salt and pepper to taste

2 ½ lb pork shoulder, cut in
1-inch cubes

2 Tbsp white vinegar

1-2 tsp sugar

caraway or dill seeds to taste

1 cup water

2 large carrots, cubed

2 potatoes, cut in large
pieces

1 large potato, grated

¾ to 1 cup sour cream

*Making good use of pork shoulder, this savory dish is
a tender and delectable entrée.*

Place the sauerkraut in a large bowl. In a large skillet,
fry the onions in oil until they begin to turn color. Add to
the sauerkraut.

Preheat oven to 350° F.

Mix together the flour, paprika, sage, salt and pepper
in a paper bag and add the pork cubes, a few at a time,
shaking the bag to coat the meat with the flour. Fry in the
skillet until browned; remove to a Dutch oven or a large
casserole. Add the sauerkraut, vinegar, sugar, salt (if
needed), and the caraway or dill seed. Add the cup of
water and cover.

Bake the meat-sauerkraut mixture for 30-45 minutes,
then stir the carrots and potatoes into the sauerkraut, and
return casserole to the oven for an hour or more, until the
meat is tender and the vegetables are cooked. Add the
grated potato, and cook for 15 minutes more. Stir in the
sour cream, and dust with a little paprika for garnish.

Sunday Sauerkraut Dinner

Company coming? You can't go wrong serving this well-dressed combination of pork and smoked meat together with some vegetables.

In a large Dutch oven, place the smoked pork shoulder roll (remove casing, if any), the pork blade roast, wine, chicken broth, the juniper berries, and the herb bouquet. Bring to a boil over high heat; reduce the heat to low, and simmer for 1 ½ hours. Discard the juniper berries and herb bouquet.

Add onions, carrots, potatoes, wieners or bratwurst, and sauerkraut in layers. Cover tightly, and simmer for another 45-50 minutes until the meat and vegetables are fork tender.

With a slotted spoon, remove the vegetables to a large, heated platter, and keep warm. Slice the meats, halve the bratwurst or wieners and arrange on another platter. Skim the fat from the pan liquid, adding some water or soup stock if insufficient liquid remains in the pan. Make a thin paste of flour and water, stir into pan juices, and let bubble for a minute or two, stirring vigorously to prevent lumping. Correct seasoning. Serve the gravy separately.

2 ½ lbs smoked pork shoulder roll

2 ½ lbs boned pork shoulder blade roast

2 cups dry wine

3 cups chicken broth

8 juniper berries or 2 Tbsp gin

Herb Bouquet No. 5 (see index)

6 medium onions, halved

4 carrots, julienned

10-12 medium potatoes

10 bratwurst or barbecue wieners

4 cups drained sauerkraut

4 Tbsp flour

water

Ham with Sauerkraut

8 slices diced salt pork, or bacon

1 large onion, diced

1 tsp sugar

4 cups sauerkraut

salt and pepper to taste

1 Tbsp white vinegar

¹/2 cup or more broth or water

2 Tbsp bread crumbs

1 ¹/2 lbs potatoes boiled whole, thickly sliced

3 carrots, cooked, sliced

3 parsnips, cooked, sliced

1 ¹/2 lbs cooked ham thinly sliced

1-2 cups sour cream

Here is another way to serve ham in a filling one-dish meal.

In a large skillet or Dutch oven, fry the diced salt pork or bacon together with the diced onion. Add sugar, sauerkraut, salt if needed, vinegar, broth or water, and simmer until tender, about 45 minutes.

Preheat oven to 300° F.

Sprinkle a large casserole dish with the bread crumbs. Put in a layer of sauerkraut mixture, then layers of potatoes, carrots, parsnips, and ham. Repeat the layers, ending with sauerkraut. Top with sour cream and bake for 30-40 minutes until heated through, and the flavors are blended.

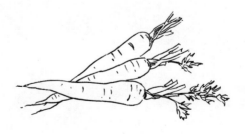

A Little Stew

Bigos (Hunter's Stew), one of the most famous of Poland's traditional dishes, is excellent for large groups. Not quite a stew, not quite a casserole dish, it is reminiscent of the French Choucroute Garni, in that it is a combination of fresh and smoked meats. It improves with reheating, and will keep refrigerated for a full week. Inspired by the Bigos, the Poles suggest an excellent way of using leftover meats. The greater the combination of meats, the better.

Cook the mushrooms. Drain, reserving liquid. Cut up the mushrooms and set aside.

Put the sauerkraut and sugar into a Dutch oven. Fry the diced bacon and onions until they are transparent; add the flour (if necessary, add a tsp of cooking oil). Stir until the flour is lightly browned. Add some of the mushroom liquid and stir until smooth. Add to the sauerkraut with the remaining mushroom liquid. Add the apples, tomatoes, and sour cream. Simmer for 1 hour. Add the chopped meats and simmer for another 25-30 minutes before serving

1 cup mushrooms

water

4 cups sauerkraut

$^1/_2$ tsp sugar (optional)

1 large onion, minced

1 Tbsp flour

2 apples, cored, diced

3-4 tomatoes, peeled, diced

3-4 cups leftover meats, chopped

$^1/_4$ cup Madeira (optional)

Suckling Pig

2 ¹/₂ lbs suckling pig, or cubed pork

water

2 cloves garlic, minced

pepper to taste

3 whole cloves

2 bay leaves

¹/₂ tsp caraway seeds

1 onion, cubed

5-6 potatoes, peeled

3 cups sauerkraut

A simple dish using a couple of pounds of suckling pig or young pork. The meat is very tender and the dish is satisfying.

Using a Dutch oven, cover the meat with water, and add garlic, pepper, whole cloves, bay leaves, and the caraway seeds. Cook for 45 minutes.

Preheat oven to 350° F.

Cut up two potatoes into small pieces and mix with the sauerkraut. In a small skillet, fry the onions lightly, and mix with sauerkraut; add the sauerkraut- onion combination to the meat. Cook for 30 minutes, stirring, until the small pieces of potatoes are blended. Quarter the remaining potatoes and place on top of the sauerkraut.

Bake the casserole for 45 minutes, or until the potatoes are cooked and beginning to brown.

Pineapple Ribs and Sauerkraut

3 lbs pork country style ribs

20-oz can sliced pineapple, drained, juice reserved

2 Tbsp brown sugar

1 medium onion, grated

2 ¹/₂ cups drained sauerkraut

¹/₃ cup soy sauce

4 tsp prepared mustard

¹/₂ cup diced celery

Pineapple and soy sauce combine to make this sauerkraut a new taste experience.

Preheat oven to 350° F.

Cut the ribs into serving-size pieces. Place the pineapple slices in a Dutch oven or a large casserole, reserving 3 slices for garnish. Combine all the remaining ingredients with the pork pieces. Toss to mix well. Bake uncovered for 1 ¹/₄ hours or until the ribs are tender. Skim off the fat. Garnish with reserved pineapple.

Pineapple Sauerkraut

4 servings

Here is another way to have a sauerkraut dish with pineapple.

In a large skillet, fry the bacon and onion in butter until translucent.

Put the sauerkraut into a large saucepan or Dutch oven; add the bacon and onion. Pour in the pineapple juice, adding enough to reach half way up the sauerkraut. Simmer until the sauerkraut is well cooked, about 1 to 1 1/2 hours. Thicken with a grated potato or a thin flour-and-water paste. Add the drained pineapple. Cook together for another 10-15 minutes, until the flavors blend.

1/2 cup diced bacon

1 large onion, diced

1-2 Tbsp butter

4 cups rinsed, drained, sauerkraut

1 can drained, cubed pineapple, juice reserved

2-3 Tbsp flour or 1 large potato, grated

Prunes, Ribs, and Kraut

6-8 servings

All sorts of fruits are good with sauerkraut. Spare ribs go very well with both.

Cut the ribs into individual portions and brown them in a Dutch oven in their own fat. Remove the ribs from the Dutch oven and reserve. Add the sauerkraut to the pan and cook over medium heat until limp. Sprinkle with brown sugar. Return the ribs to the pot with the whole cloves. Add sauerkraut juice or water to just barely cover.

Simmer on top of the stove for about 1 1/2 hours. Add the dried or fresh fruit, and continue cooking for another hour, or until the meat is very tender.

Variation: For a one-dish supper, you can add carrot slices and large cubes of potatoes for the last 45-50 minutes cooking time.

4 lbs spare ribs

4 cups drained sauerkraut, juice reserved

brown sugar to taste

3 whole cloves

dried prunes, raisins, or pears, or fresh apples and pears

Sauerkraut and Apricot Casserole

2 Tbsp cooking oil

1 cup diced onions

4 cups rinsed, drained sauerkraut

2 jars (7 ¹/₂-oz each) strained apricots for babies

3 large pork steaks, cut in half, or 6 pork chops

¹/₂ tsp celery salt

¹/₂ tsp lemon pepper

6 pinches of sage

¹/₄ to ¹/₂ cup meat juices, reserved from cooking

Sauerkraut and apricots may sound like an unlikely combination, but the flavor is excellent.

Preheat oven to 350° F.

Heat oil in a large skillet and sauté onions for 5 minutes. In a medium-sized casserole, combine the sauerkraut, apricots, onions, and sugar.

Brown the pork steaks or chops in the remaining oil in the skillet. Sprinkle each steak with lemon pepper, celery salt, and a pinch of sage. Arrange over the sauerkraut. Pour a half cup of water into the skillet and loosen the browned bits from the meat. Pour ¹/₄ to ¹/₂ cup of this water over the pork steaks.

Bake the casserole for 30 minutes, then lower heat to 300° F and continue baking for another hour, or until the meat is tender.

4-6 servings

Sweet Sauerkraut

3 cups sauerkraut

7 medium tomatoes, chopped

2 cups tomato soup

1 cup raisins

2 stalks celery, diced

1 onion, minced

4 Tbsp brown sugar

¹/₂ cup chopped prunes (optional)

This Israeli dish cannot be hurried, as it depends on long, slow cooking for the development of its special flavor.

Incorporate all ingredients in a heavy pot or a Dutch oven with a tightly fitting lid. Simmer on very low heat for at least 6 hours.

Cubed Beef and Sauerkraut

6-8 servings

Although pork is used in many sauerkraut recipes, beef is more than adequate, especially if you are using economical cuts which require long, slow cooking.

Using a large non-stick skillet, brown the beef cubes in hot oil. Add the onions. Sprinkle with pepper, garlic salt, paprika, and the powdered garlic. Add the salt to taste. Cover, and continue cooking slowly over low heat for about 30 minutes.

Preheat oven to 325°-350° F.

Stir the sauerkraut into the contents of the skillet. Add the bay leaves, the whole cloves, and the boiling water. Turn the skillet contents into a Dutch oven or a casserole dish, and bake for another hour and a half, or until the meat is very tender.

3 lbs chuck roast, cut in 2-inch cubes

2 Tbsp cooking oil

3 onions, chopped

$1/2$ tsp pepper

$1/2$ tsp garlic salt

1 tsp paprika

salt to taste

1 Tbsp garlic powder

4 cups sauerkraut

2 bay leaves

3-4 whole cloves

1 cup boiling water

Beef Platter with Sauerkraut

4 lbs boneless beef, rump or chuck roast

1 cup water

1 envelope onion soup mix

$^{1}/_{2}$ cup chili sauce

1 Tbsp chili sauce

1 tsp chopped dill

1 Tbsp paprika

$^{1}/_{2}$ tsp pepper

3 cups sauerkraut

$^{1}/_{4}$ cup firmly packed brown sugar

1 jalapeño pepper, finely chopped

1 cup sour cream

Various less expensive cuts of beef may be tenderized through long, slow cooking when they are used with sauerkraut.

In a Dutch oven, brown the roast on all sides in its own fat. Remove the fat. Add water, onion soup mix, chili sauce, dill, paprika, and pepper to the meat. Cover.

Simmer on the stove top or cook in a preheated oven at 325° F for about two hours until the meat is almost tender.

Mix the sauerkraut with the sugar and jalapeño pepper. Place around the roast, and cook for another hour or until the meat is very tender. Lift the roast from the pan and set on a carving board, covered with foil to keep it warm.

Stir $^{1}/_{2}$ cup of sauerkraut into the sour cream; then stir the sauerkraut-cream mixture into the remaining sauerkraut in the pan. Heat gently until hot enough to serve, but do not bring to a boil. Spoon the sauerkraut onto a serving platter. Carve the meat into thick slices and place on top of the sauerkraut. Serve with hot buttered noodles.

Stuffed Steak

4 servings

Stuffed meats are delicious and attractive. Here is a steak with a novel stuffing.

Season both sides of the steak with celery salt, pepper, and powdered garlic.

In a large skillet, sauté the onion and celery using the butter or oil. Add sauerkraut and without further cooking, moisten with sour cream.

Preheat oven to 350° F.

Top the seasoned steak with 3 strips of bacon and then with the sauerkraut mixture. Cover the stuffing with the remaining slices of bacon. Roll up, tie with string, and place in a roasting pan. Bake for afout 1 hour until the steak is tender, covering the pan if the steak begins to brown too soon. Slice to serve.

1 large round steak

celery salt

pepper

powdered garlic

1 onion, chopped

¹/₂ cup diced celery

3 cups drained sauerkraut

2 Tbsp butter or oil

2-3 Tbsp sour cream

6 slices bacon

Steak Sauerkraut Supper

4 servings

Here is another way to cook steak. A bit of steak sauce gives it real zest.

Season the steaks with garlic salt, pepper, and celery seed. Heat the oil in a skillet and fry the onion until soft. Add the steaks, and fry until they are brown and tender, about 5 minutes, turning once and stirring the onion frequently. Remove the steaks and onion to a platter; brush with the steak sauce; keep warm.

Using the drippings in the pan, fry the potatoes over low heat until they are lightly browned, adding more oil if needed. Stir in the sauerkraut and the ¹/₂ tsp sugar, or to taste. Cook until the sauerkraut is softened and heated through, stirring in the brown bits from the bottom of the skillet. Arrange the steaks, potatoes, and sauerkraut on a platter.

1 ¹/₂ lbs cubed beef steaks

garlic salt

pepper

¹/₂ tsp celery seed

1-2 Tbsp cooking oil

1 medium onion, diced

1 Tbsp commercial steak sauce

4 medium potatoes, cooked, quartered

2 ¹/₂ cups drained sauerkraut

¹/₂ tsp sugar

Baked Corned Beef Hash

3 cups rinsed, drained sauerkraut

1 large onion

6 whole cloves

1 chicken bouillon cube

1 1/2 cups water

1/4 tsp dried thyme

1/4 tsp Italian spice

1/2 tsp oregano

12-oz can corned beef, chopped fine

1 can tomato mushroom sauce

2 tsp prepared horseradish

1 tsp dry mustard

2 apples, cored, sliced 1 1/4-inch thick

Corned beef is delicious in this version of an old favorite.

Using a medium-sized saucepan, place sauerkraut, together with the whole onion studded with cloves, the bouillon cube dissolved in the water, thyme, the Italian spice, and oregano. Simmer for 30-45 minutes, then discard the onion. Turn the sauerkraut mixture into an ovenproof dish.

Preheat oven to 375°-400° F.

Combine the corned beef with the tomato mushroom sauce, the horseradish, and the dry mustard. Spread on top of the sauerkraut mixture. Arrange the apple slices on top. Bake for 30 minutes until piping hot.

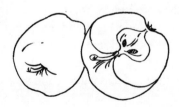

Rudie's Casserole

5-6 servings

Preheat oven to 350° F.

Using a 1 ½ quart casserole, place the sauerkraut on the bottom, and cover with the corned beef slices. Top with the shredded cheese. Mix the dressings and spread over the first two layers. Arrange the tomato slices on top.

Melt the butter or margarine, mix with the bread crumbs, and sprinkle over the top of the casserole. Bake for 45-60 minutes until heated thoroughly.

3 cups partially drained sauerkraut

12-oz can corned beef, sliced

2 cups shredded Swiss, Cheddar, or Monterey Jack cheese

½ cup mayonnaise

½ cup Thousand Island

2 medium tomatoes, sliced

2 Tbsp margarine or butter

¼ cup bread crumbs

Polish Sausage Bake

4 servings

Smoked meats of all kinds are a natural choice with sauerkraut. This recipe, inspired by Polish cooks, makes use of Polish sausage, but kielbasa or a Ukrainian-style garlic sausage could be used with equal success.

Preheat oven to 350° F.

Mix the sauerkraut with the onions, basil, and celery seed. Put into a 2-quart casserole. Wash the sausage, deeply slashing it at 1-inch intervals, push the sausage down into the sauerkraut. Dissolve the brown sugar in the hot water and drizzle over the sauerkraut and sausage. Cover.

Bake for about an hour until the sausage is hot and the sauerkraut is tender.

3 cups drained sauerkraut

½ cup chopped onions

1 ½ tsp dried basil

½ tsp celery seed

1 Polish sausage ring

2-3 Tbsp brown sugar

1 cup hot water

One-Dish Supper

3 cups sauerkraut, rinsed, partially drained

1/2 cup diced bacon

1/2 cup chopped onion

1 sausage ring cut in 1/4-inch slices

2 cups, or more, fluffy, mashed potatoes

1/2 tsp nutmeg

butter or margarine

1/2 cup dried bread crumbs

Here is a quick dish reminiscent of shepherd's pie. Meat and vegetables are topped with fluffy potatoes. Serve with a green salad and a few pickles for a complete meal.

Preheat oven to 350° F.

Grease a 1 1/2-qt casserole and place the sauerkraut in it. Fry the bacon and onions together until partly cooked. Add to the sauerkraut and stir. Arrange the sausage slices over the top. Cover with the mashed potatoes. Sprinkle with nutmeg and dot with butter. Cover with bread crumbs.

Bake for 40-60 minutes until nicely browned.

Sauerkraut Alsace Style

4 Tbsp butter

2 carrots, diced

1 cup onion, chopped

1 parsnip, chopped

5 cups rinsed, drained sauerkraut, squeezed dry

2 garlic sausage, 2 lbs each or other smoked sausage

4 cups beef stock

1 cup dry vermouth

1 Herb Bouquet No. 3 (see index)

Alsatians add dry vermouth to this dish for extra flavor.

Preheat oven to 325°-350° F.

Melt the butter in a Dutch oven, add the carrots, onions, and parsnip. Sauté gently until the vegetables are partly cooked. Add the sauerkraut and stir to mix. Add the sausage. Pour in the stock and wine. Cover tightly. Bake for 2 1/2 to 3 hours or until the liquid has been absorbed, adding the herb bouquet after the first 1 1/2 hours. Discard the herb bouquet before serving. Serve with crusty buns.

Supper Special

This is a complete supper dish, dressed up well enough for guests. It uses pork cutlets, ham, and spicy sausages.

Using a large casserole dish or a Dutch oven, line the bottom with 6 thick slices of bacon. Top with sauerkraut; the cutlets; the onions, each of which is studded with 2 whole cloves; the herb bouquet; and the smoked sausages. Lay 6 thick slices of bacon slices over all. Pour in the wine and stock. Cover tightly. Bring to a boil, reduce heat, and simmer for at least 2 hours. Add the wieners and ham, and continue simmering for another 20 minutes.

Serve the sauerkraut in the middle of a large platter surrounded by the meats and the rolled slices of ham. Serve buttered potatoes and carrots between the meats.

12 thick slices bacon

5 cups sauerkraut

6 smoked pork cutlets

3 onions

1 Herb Bouquet No. 3 (see index)

10 slices cooked ham, rolled

10 smoked sausages or fresh spiced sausages

1 small bottle white wine

3-4 cups stock

10 wieners

Pickles and Kraut—Polish Style

Polish cuisine suggests yet another way to use smoked meats and pickles.

In a casserole or Dutch oven, simmer the sauerkraut with the bouillon, herb bouquet, butter, onion, and the salt and pepper. Stir frequently and cook about 45 minutes or until the sauerkraut is just soft, adding more bouillon if necessary. Add the dill pickle slices. Remove the herb bouquet. Five minutes before serving, add the sour cream and flour. Stir, and allow to bubble up once more.

4 cups sauerkraut, squeezed dry

1 cup bouillon

1 Herb Bouquet No. 5 (see index)

2 Tbsp butter

1 onion, minced

salt and pepper to taste

4 dill pickles, thinly sliced

3-4 Tbsp sour cream

2 Tbsp flour

Pickles and Sauerkraut, Hungarian Style

6 cups chopped sauerkraut

salt and pepper to taste

4-5 cups stock

¹/₃ cup diced salt pork

3 onions, chopped

2 cloves garlic, crushed

1 lb sausage, peeled, sliced

5 pickles, sliced

1 Tbsp paprika

3 Tbsp tomato purée

3 peppercorns

caraway seeds to taste

3 medium potatoes, peeled and grated

In a Dutch oven, cook the sauerkraut with the salt and pepper and stock until soft, about 1 ¹/₂ hours.

In a large, non-stick skillet, fry the salt pork with the onions and the garlic. Add to the sauerkraut together with the sausage, pickles, paprika, tomato pure, the peppercorns, and the caraway seeds. Stir in the grated potatoes and simmer for another 20-25 minutes.

Farmer's Pork Supper

Beer is a great tenderizer. Here it is used to give flavor to pork chops and sauerkraut for a great supper dish.

Preheat oven to 350° F.

Grease a 13-inch by 9-inch baking pan. In a large non-stick skillet, fry the onion, celery, and carrot slices for 3 minutes in the butter. Add the salt, thyme, oregano, dill seeds, caraway seeds, and the sauerkraut; sauté for 5 minutes. Add the apple slices and cook for 3 minutes more. Add the 6 cups of bread cubes and stir well. Put all these ingredients into the baking dish. Set aside.

Trim the fat off the pork chops. Place the fat into the skillet and render enough fat over low heat to brown the pork chops on both sides. Place the browned chops on top of the sauerkraut mixture; pour the beer over all. Cover well with aluminium foil; bake for 1 to 1 ¹/₂ hours until the meat is tender.

¹/₄ *cup butter*

¹/₂ *cup onion, diced*

¹/₄ *cup celery, diced*

1 large carrot, sliced

¹/₂ *tsp salt*

¹/₂ *tsp dried thyme*

1 tsp oregano

¹/₂ *tsp dill seed*

¹/₂ *tsp caraway seed*

3 cups sauerkraut

1 apple, peeled and sliced

1 loaf Italian bread cut into 1-inch cubes (6 cups)

6 pork chops, ³/₄-inch thick

¹/₂ *cup beer*

Kapusta (Cabbage)

1 cup dry kidney beans

5 cups ham stock

4 cups rinsed, drained sauerkraut

1 Herb Bouquet No. 2 (see index)

¹/₂ cup chopped celery

1 carrot, diced

10-oz can undrained mushrooms

1 Tbsp fresh or dry dill

1 cup peas, fresh or frozen

1 tsp salt

¹/₂ tsp pepper

1 onion, chopped

3 Tbsp flour

3-4 Tbsp butter

The Ukrainians have their own way of preparing sauerkraut and beans. This recipe differs from the previous one, as it uses more vegetables, and is finished with a brown flour gravy. This dish freezes well.

Soak the beans overnight. Drain the beans in the morning, and cover them with fresh, cold water; bring to a boil, and boil for one minute. Rinse to remove foam; cover again with cold water, bring to a boil, reduce heat, and simmer on low heat until the beans are very tender. Drain and mash. Set aside.

Put ham stock into a large pot and bring to a boil; add the sauerkraut, herb bouquet, celery, and carrots. Bring to a boil, reduce heat and simmer for 30 minutes. Add the mushrooms, dill, peas, and seasoning. Taste before adding the salt. Simmer for another 30 minutes.

In a non-stick skillet, melt the butter and brown the onion and flour. Add some broth to the flour, stirring vigorously to make a smooth paste. Add to the broth. Return to a boil and simmer for another 30 minutes more to cook the flour. Serve hot.

Israeli Sauerkraut

4 servings

This Israeli recipe makes use of smoked meats. For an authentic dish, use kosher margarine and purchase the sausages from a Jewish butcher.

Using a non-stick skillet, melt the margarine, add the onions and celery. Fry over moderate heat until the vegetables begin to change color. Add the remaining ingredients, except the smoked sausages, and cook on low heat for about 45 minutes. Add the smoked sausage and cook until well heated.

1 Tbsp margarine

1 cup chopped onions

$^1/_2$ cup chopped celery

4 cups sauerkraut

$^1/_4$ tsp black pepper

$^1/_2$ tsp caraway

$^1/_2$ tsp paprika

1 tsp sugar

$^1/_2$ cup water

8 smoked sausages

Sour-Creamy Supper

6-8 servings

This recipe makes use of sour cream, but the flavor will be just as tasty if you use sweet cream instead.

In a medium-sized non-stick skillet, fry the bacon and onion in the margarine or butter until the onion starts to change color and the bacon is almost cooked. Put the sauerkraut in a medium-sized pot and add the onion and bacon. Cover. Simmer for an hour, if necessary adding a little water. When cooked, uncover, drain off the remaining liquid, add pepper and salt to taste. Stir in the cream just before serving.

$^1/_2$ cup diced bacon

1 onion, chopped

3 Tbsp butter or margarine

3 cups sauerkraut

salt and pepper to taste

5 Tbsp sour cream.

Bean or Pea Purée with Sauerkraut

6 servings

6 cups rinsed, drained
sauerkraut

1 Tbsp cooking oil

1 large onion, diced

$^{1}/_{2}$ cup diced bacon

3 bay leaves

4 whole cloves

8 peppercorns

6-8 juniper berries

2 medium apples, cored,
diced

1 tsp paprika

1 Tbsp caraway or dill seed

1 large potato, grated

3 cups stock

6 fresh or smoked pork hocks

cooked beans or puréed peas
(recipes follow)

In Germany, beans, peas, and lentils are served with sauerkraut. While the ingredients in this recipe are similar to those in the previous dish, the flavor is quite different because juniper berries have been used.

Put the sauerkraut into a large casserole or Dutch oven. In a medium-sized skillet, fry the onion and bacon in the oil until they begin to change color. Add to the sauerkraut. Make a herb bouquet of the bay leaves, cloves, peppercorns, and juniper berries. Add to the pot along with the diced apples, paprika, and the caraway or dill seeds, and grated potato. Add enough stock to half cover the sauerkraut. Put the pork hocks into the sauerkraut and simmer for 1 $^{1}/_{2}$ to 2 hours until the meat is tender but not falling apart. Discard the herb bouquet after the first hour.

To serve, heap a portion of sauerkraut onto a plate. Top with a pork hock and add a serving of beans or pea purée (see below).

Bean or Pea Purée
with Sauerkraut

(continued)

Beans, Dried Peas, or Lentil Purée

Soak beans, peas, or lentils overnight. In the morning, drain off the water. Place the beans, peas, or lentils in a medium-sized pot and cover with fresh water. Bring to the boil, and boil 1 minute. Reduce heat. Add all the diced vegetables, except the onion, with 1 tsp salt, and simmer until the beans and vegetables are well cooked.

In a medium-sized non-stick skillet, fry the onions and bacon until both are just beginning to change color. Add the flour, and brown together to a medium dark shade. Add some of the stock from the pot (or water) to the flour, stir vigorously to make a smooth paste. Add to the beans and vegetables. Cook for 10 minutes longer until the dish is thickened.

Puréed Peas

Peas, green or split, are cooked as above, although some liquid may remain and should be drained off. Purée the peas through a sieve or in a blender. Put the purée into a shallow baking dish. Top with fried onions and bacon. Bake in a 350° F oven for about 20 minutes, or until lightly browned. Serve alongside the sauerkraut and pork hock.

2 cups dried white beans, green split peas, or lentils

1 large carrot, diced

1 parsnip, diced

¹/₂ celery root, diced

2 stalks celery, diced

1 tsp salt

1 onion, diced

¹/₂ cup diced bacon

2-3 Tbsp butter

2 Tbsp flour

6 servings

Red Kidney Beans and Sauerkraut

³/₄ cup dry red kidney beans or two 10-oz cans red kidney beans

4 pork hocks

4-6 whole cloves

4 bay leaves

4 cups sauerkraut

A Yugoslavian friend described with some nostalgia a sauerkraut dish his mother used to cook. After questioning him closely, I created this recipe. He said it was "pretty close to the real thing."

Soak the beans overnight. In the morning, pour off the water they soaked in. Fill a medium-sized pot with fresh, cold water; bring the beans to a boil, and boil for one minute. Reduce heat, and simmer slowly for an hour or more, until they are cooked. Drain.

Using a Dutch oven, cover the pork hocks with water. Add the bay leaves and the whole cloves (tied in cheesecloth for easy removal). Simmer slowly for about 3 hours until the pork hocks are well cooked. Remove the hocks, bay leaves, and cloves, and strain the stock. Add the sauerkraut to the stock, and cook for about 45 minutes.

Meanwhile, remove the skin and bones from the hocks, and cut the meat into bite-size pieces. Add the beans and meat to the sauerkraut. Stir, then heat through. Serve hot with mashed potatoes and buttered carrots

Creamed Rice and Sauerkraut

6 servings

As far back as I can remember, my mother cooked sauerkraut with fresh cream. Although she prepared it in other ways as well, this remained our favorite. Mother used fresh dairy cream, but commercial whipping cream is a good substitute, although you may wish to use half-and-half cream if calories are a factor. Mother served this dish sometimes as a main dish, and at other times as a side dish.

Put the meat into a large pot; cover with cold water; add the bay leaves and cloves. Bring to a boil, skim, and simmer for 2 hours, until the meat is tender. Add the sauerkraut and simmer for 30 minutes. Put in the rice, and stir well. Add water if necessary. Keep the pot covered while the rice is cooking. When the rice is cooked, the stock should be reduced completely. Drain, if necessary. Add the cream, stirring well. Do not boil again.

The dish should be thick. You can serve the meat as a separate dish or cut it up and return it to the pot.

Serve with fluffy, mashed potatoes, fresh peas, and rye bread or crusty rolls. Homemade bread is even better.

4 large or 6 small pork hocks, or 2-3 lbs lean spareribs

3-4 bay leaves

4-5 whole cloves

4 cups drained sauerkraut

³/₄ cup washed rice

³/₄ to 1 pint of half-and-half cream, or whipping cream

Vegetable Supper

3 medium carrots, sliced

1/2 cup diced celery root

1/2 cup chopped celery

1 large sweet green pepper
diced

1 large onion, diced

1 jalapeño pepper, minced

1/2 cup diced turnip

3 cups sauerkraut

1/2 cup washed rice

2 cups sweet cream

Sweet cream is used often in sauerkraut recipes. Half-and-half is suggested here, but if you like the richness of cream, use whipping cream. If you are calorie-conscious, you could use milk, but you will lose some of the rich flavor.

Put all the vegetables—including the jalapeño pepper—except the sauerkraut, into a medium-sized pot. Add enough water to cover the vegetables. Bring to a boil, reduce the temperature, and simmer 10 minutes. Add the sauerkraut and more water if needed. Simmer for another 20-25 minutes, until the vegetables are cooked, making sure they are still covered with water. Add the rice to the vegetables. Stir just enough to incorporate the rice. Bring to a boil, reduce heat, then simmer for another 15-20 minutes for the rice to cook. If the water is not absorbed, drain. Then add the sweet cream. Use as a side dish or the main course.

Saturday Special

3 slices bacon or ham, sliced

1 cup diced celery

2 cups chopped onion

1 cup sliced carrots

1/2 cup diced green peppers

3 cups drained sauerkraut

3 potatoes, cut into 1-inch
cubes

2 Golden Delicious apples,
cut into small chunks

Here's a quickly prepared and cooked supper dish. Golden Delicious apples are used in it to give a hint of sweetness.

In a large skillet, fry the bacon or ham until it begins to lose some fat. Discard all but 2 Tbsp drippings from the pan. Add the celery, onion, carrots, and green peppers. cook over medium heat until tender-crisp. Stir in the remaining ingredients and continue simmering until the vegetables are cooked, 15-20 minutes.

Bavarian Style Baked Squash

4-6 servings

Stuffed squash is always special. Here is dainty butternut or acorn squash filled with a satisfying stuffing made of meat and sauerkraut.

Preheat oven to 350°-375° F.

Cook prepared squash in an uncovered shallow pan in a small amount of water until tender, 20-25 minutes. Scoop out the pulp into a large bowl, reserving the shells. Add to the meat, garlic, savory, mustard, curry, salt and pepper, mixing well. In a large non-stick skillet, fry the meat until cooked. Add to the pulp, together with the bread crumbs, the brown sugar and the sauerkraut. Mix well. Pile the pulp-meat mixture lightly into the shells. Place into a baking dish, and bake for 20-25 minutes.

3 butternut or acorn squash, halved lengthwise, seeded

³/₄ lb lean hamburger or sausage meat

1 clove garlic, crushed

³/₄ tsp savory

³/₄ tsp mustard

¹/₄ tsp curry powder

¹/₄ tsp or more pepper

¹/₂ tsp salt

1 ¹/₂ cups soft bread crumbs

1 Tbsp brown sugar

2 cups drained sauerkraut

Apple Kraut

6 servings

This is a dish for a busy day—it can be prepared in less than 1 hour.

Melt butter or fat in a large non-stick skillet and add the flour. Stir until smooth. Add the sauerkraut, onions, vinegar, cloves, bay leaves, brown sugar, and the water. Cover and simmer for 30-40 minutes. Add the chopped apples in the last 10 minutes of cooking.

¹/₄ cup butter or bacon fat

2 Tbsp flour

3 cups drained sauerkraut

6 green onions, chopped

¹/₄ cup vinegar

4 whole cloves

2 bay leaves

2 Tbsp brown sugar

¹/₄ cup water

2 apples, cored, diced

Lunch at Grandma's

1 ¹/₂ lbs sausage meat

1 egg

¹/₂ cup bread crumbs

³/₄ tsp dry mustard

³/₄ tsp sage

¹/₄ tsp curry

¹/₂ tsp powdered ginger

salt and pepper to taste

butter or margarine

6 medium potatoes, unpeeled

3 or more onions, chopped

3 cups drained sauerkraut

garlic butter (recipe follows)

thick slices rye bread

2 tomatoes, sliced

For a very informal supper or lunch, here is a recipe which can be doubled or tripled with no trouble. Add any other ingredients you like.

In a large bowl, mix the meat, egg, bread crumbs, mustard, sage, curry, ginger, pepper, and about ¹/₂ tsp salt. Shape into cakes about ¹/₂ to ³/₄ inches thick, and fry in butter or margarine until browned on both sides. Set aside. Boil the washed potatoes in salted water. Drain, cool and slice ¹/₄ inch thick.

Fry the onions in 1 Tbsp of butter or margarine. Remove and set aside. Fry the potatoes lightly in the butter. Remove from the pan. Add more margarine or butter to the skillet if necessary, and fry the sauerkraut until it begins to change color.

Spread the rye bread with garlic butter and broil until it begins to brown.

Serve on the garlic bread with tomato slices.

Garlic Butter

¹/₂ lb butter or margarine, softened

2 cloves garlic, minced or very finely grated

Mix the two ingredients together and let stand for at least an hour for the flavors to blend. Garlic butter will keep in a covered container in the refrigerator for several weeks.

Garnished Sauerkraut

Wines and spirits are sometimes added to, or used in place of soup stock or water. This French recipe uses wine and juniper berries, or gin for a distinctive flavor.

In a large skillet, sauté the onions and chopped celery in the bacon fat until tender. Add the sauerkraut and fry for another 10 minutes. Transfer the ingredients into a Dutch oven. Add the apples, peppercorns, and juniper berries or gin. Pour in the white wine. Cook slowly for about 1 1/4 hours.

Meanwhile, in a small saucepan, cover the link sausages with cold water, bring to a boil, and let simmer for 5-6 minutes. Pour off the water and brown lightly in a pan with a small amount of oil to prevent sticking. Add with the other meats and the herb bouquet to the sauerkraut mixture and cook for another 35-40 minutes, or until the chops are tender. Discard the peppercorns, herb bouquet, and the juniper berries.

To serve, mound the sauerkraut in the middle of the platter and surround it with the cooked meats.

3 medium onions, diced

1/2 cup chopped celery

2 Tbsp bacon fat

3 cups rinsed and drained sauerkraut

2 tart apples, peeled and diced

6 peppercorns

10 juniper berries or 1/4 cup gin

2 1/2 cups white wine

12 link sausages

2 Tbsp cooking oil

Herb Bouquet No. 4 (see index)

1 lb garlic sausage, peeled, cut into 1/2-inch pieces

6 slices ham, sliced 1/4 inch thick

6 smoked pork chops

6 wieners

Choucroute Garni

6 ham hocks

4 cups sauerkraut, soaked in
cold water and drained

2 cups dry wine

3 bay leaves

6 medium carrots, cut
lengthwise and quartered

1 medium onion, peeled

6 whole cloves

1 $^1/_2$ lb knackwurst

2 red apples, cored and sliced

12 new potatoes

Ham hocks, smoked sausage, and new potatoes combine to make this handsome and hearty meal.

Add the ham hocks to a Dutch oven with the sauerkraut, wine, bay leaves, and carrots. Stud the onion with cloves and push it down into the sauerkraut. Heat to boiling, reduce heat, and simmer for 1 $^1/_2$ hours, stirring occasionally, until the ham hocks are nearly tender.

Score the knackwurst in a few places and put on top of the sauerkraut mixture along with the apple. Cook for another 10 minutes. Meanwhile, cook the potatoes separately in salted water. Drain well.

Place the sauerkraut and carrots in the middle of a larger platter. Surround the sauerkraut with potatoes and the meats. Serve with rye bread. Mustard or a mustard pickle goes well with this one.

Gourmet Special

This complete dinner, served on a large platter, is a colorful gourmet special for your guests.

Cut the Bavarian smokies in half lengthwise. Brown them lightly in cooking oil in a large skillet or Dutch oven. Brown the sausage slices. Set the sausages aside on a large plate.

Sauté the apples and pears in butter for 4-5 minutes until golden brown. Add to reserved sausages. Add more butter to the Dutch oven and add the onion, garlic, carrots, parsnip, celery, potatoes, thyme, and sauté until crisp- tender.

Add sausages, half the sautéed apples and pear rings, sauerkraut, the pork shoulder roll, apple juice, wine, juniper berries, and ground cloves. Cover and simmer for 45-60 minutes until the vegetables are tender, and the pork shoulder is cooked.

To serve, heap the sauerkraut in the middle of the large platter. Slice the pork shoulder roll and place it and other meats on top of the sauerkraut. Surround with the vegetables, and the remaining apple and pear slices.

6 Bavarian smokies

1 Tbsp cooking oil

$1/2$ lb sausage, sliced

2 green apples, cored, sliced into $1/4$-inch thick rings

2 red pears, cored, sliced into $1/4$-inch-thick rings

2 Tbsp butter

1 large red onion, sliced

2 cloves garlic, minced

2 bunches baby carrots

1 large parsnip cut into rounds

$1/2$ cup chopped celery

3 lbs small new red potatoes

1 Tbsp fresh or 1 tsp dried thyme

3 cups sauerkraut

1 smoked pork shoulder roll

$1/2$ cup apple juice

$1/2$ cup white wine

1 Tbsp juniper berries

1 tsp ground cloves

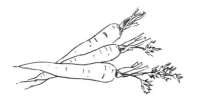

Festive Choucroute

1 lb salt pork, sliced, or 1 large bacon rind, or 1 lb bacon, thickly sliced

8 cups sauerkraut, rinsed and drained

2 Herb Bouquet No. 3(see index)

salt and pepper to taste

6 juniper berries

2 Spanish onions, sliced

5 cloves garlic, minced

champagne or white wine to cover

6 lb lean pork roast

1 pepperoni sausage

4-8 smoked sausages(chorizo, wieners, garlic sausage)

12 or more potatoes

sour cream to taste

chives to taste

bacon, fried and crumbled for garnish

Another version of Choucroute Garni makes use of champagne as the cooking liquid. The original recipe calls for salt pork as a lining for the cooking pot, but bacon rind works well, as do thick slices of bacon, which may even provide a better flavor.

Preheat oven to 275°-300° F.

Line a large, deep casserole dish or a Dutch oven with salt pork slices, bacon rinds, or thick bacon rashers. Top with half the sauerkraut as well as the herb bouquet and slab of bacon. Sprinkle generously with pepper and correct the salt. Add juniper berries, onion, minced garlic, then the rest of the sauerkraut. Cover with champagne. Cover with a tightly fitting lid and bake for 3 hours. Add the pork roast; continue cooking for 1 hour. Add the assorted sausages, and cook for a further 2 hours. Remove herb bouquet.

Meanwhile, scrub the potatoes, brush lightly with oil, and wrap in foil. Put to bake in the oven when the sausages are added to the sauerkraut. Serve the baked potatoes with sour cream, chopped chives, and fried, crumbled bacon.

Serve the sauerkraut on a large platter surrounded by the sausages and slices of pork.

Viennese Sauerkraut

4 servings

The Viennese have several ways of using wine with sauerkraut.

Melt the butter or bacon fat in a Dutch oven and sauté the onion, celery, and garlic until tender. Discard the garlic. Add the sauerkraut, the wine, and the caraway seeds. Simmer for 1 hour. Add grated potato and cook for another 30 minutes.

2 Tbsp butter or bacon fat

1 large onion, diced

$^1/_2$ cup chopped celery

1 clove garlic

3 cups sauerkraut

$^3/_4$ cup white wine

$^1/_2$ tsp caraway seeds

1 large potato, grated

Polish-Style Wine Sauerkraut

6 servings

The Viennese were not alone in recognizing the flavor wine imparts to sauerkraut. Here is a Polish version of wine-flavored sauerkraut.

In a heavy casserole or Dutch oven, simmer the sauerkraut, the wine, butter, onion, and the seasonings for 1 hour, covered. Dust with the flour, add the Maggi, and sweeten to taste with sugar. Mix thoroughly. Allow to cook for another 10-15 minutes, uncovered.

4 cups sauerkraut, squeezed dry

1 cup dry white wine

2 Tbsp butter

1 medium onion, minced

3 bay leaves

4 whole cloves

1 Tbsp dried parsley

salt and pepper to taste

1 Tbsp flour

$^1/_2$ tsp Maggi or Kitchen Bouquet

sugar to taste

Thanksgiving Sauerkraut

4 cups sauerkraut

1 tsp caraway seeds

$^1/_2$ tsp dry mustard

5 peppercorns

$^1/_2$ cup or more port wine

1 tsp fresh horseradish

5-6 green onions with tops

1 Tbsp sugar

In some parts of North America, this dish is a traditional accompaniment to Thanksgiving dinner. The fresh horseradish gives a sharp tang, excellent with turkey, chicken, or other meats.

Combine all the ingredients in a Dutch oven. Cover and bring to a boil. Reduce heat and simmer for at least 2 hours.

4-6 servings

Spruced-Up Sauerkraut

1 Tbsp cooking oil or lard

bacon rinds

12 juniper berries

Herb Bouquet No. 3
(see index)

$^1/_2$ cup sliced onions

2-3 carrots, sliced

1 small parsnip, diced

4 cups rinsed, drained
sauerkraut

2 cups stewed tomatoes,
crushed if whole

$^1/_2$ cup soup stock

This dish will acquire a completely different flavor if the tomatoes are omitted.

Grease a large casserole and line with bacon rinds.
Add the juniper berries to the herb bouquet.
Top the bacon rinds with the onions, carrots, and parsnip. Mix the sauerkraut and tomatoes, and add to the dish. Place the juniper berries and the herb bouquet in the middle. Moisten with a small amount of soup stock.

Cover and bring to a boil. Lower the heat and simmer for at least 3 hours. Remove the spices before serving. May be served with rice and slices of roast beef.

Hot Sauerkraut and Dumplings

4 servings

Use as many hot peppers as you like in this dish, but remember that the pepper seeds are hotter and spicier than the pepper flesh.

Using a medium-sized Dutch oven, add all the ingredients except the hot peppers. Cover, bring to a boil, reduce heat and simmer for 1 hour. Add the hot peppers and simmer, covered, for another 15 minutes, adding a little water if necessary.

All-purpose Dumplings

Sift together the flour, baking powder, and salt. Beat the egg lightly and add it to the dry ingredients with sufficient milk to make soft dough. Drop the dough by teaspoonfuls into the boiling sauerkraut. Cover tightly, and cook the dumplings until they are light and fluffy.

4 cups rinsed, drained sauerkraut

4-5 peppercorns

1 onion, diced

1 clove garlic, minced

1-2 hot green peppers

All-purpose Dumplings (recipe follows)

2 cups flour

$1/2$ tsp baking powder

$1/2$ tsp salt

1 egg

$1/2$ cup milk

Hamburger Supper

1 lb lean hamburger

2 cups sauerkraut

season to taste

1-2 Tbsp butter

¹/₂ cup chopped onions

3-4 cups cut-up vegetables (2 pkgs pre-cut veggies)

Hamburger or ground meat reaches our tables in many guises. Here is a quickly cooked supper that needs very little preparation. This dish can easily be expanded—just add a little more of everything.

Put all the ingredients into a saucepan. Simmer until well cooked, about 45-60 minutes, adding a little water when necessary.

Hamburger and Rice Casserole

1 lb lean ground beef

1 lb ground pork

3 Tbsp butter

1 tsp paprika

1 tsp savory

1 tsp garlic salt

2 medium onions, chopped

¹/₂ cup washed rice

4 cups rinsed, drained sauerkraut

1 apple, cored, chopped

1 Tbsp flour

1 pint sour cream

This casserole is complete in itself, but a tossed salad with your favorite vinaigrette will add a nice touch.

In a large skillet, fry the beef and pork in 1 Tbsp butter until the meats lose their color; add the paprika, savory, garlic salt, and half the chopped onion. Set mixture aside.

In a small skillet, melt 1 Tbsp butter, add the rice and the remaining onion, and sauté until the rice begins to turn golden. Turn the rice-onion mixture into a small saucepan and add 1 cup hot water. Cover and bring to a boil, reduce heat, and simmer 10 minutes, or until the rice has absorbed the liquid. Set aside.

In a large skillet, fry the sauerkraut in the remaining 1 Tbsp butter for a few minutes, add the apple, and water to allow the sauerkraut to simmer for 1 hour. The mixture should be thick. At the end of one hour, remove sauerkraut mixture from heat, sprinkle with 1 Tbsp flour, and combine well.

Preheat oven to 350° F.

Using a deep casserole, layer the reserved mixtures, repeating until the ingredients are used up. Spread with sour cream. Bake for 40-45 minutes. Serve hot.

Szegedin Goulash

The Hungarians are fond of a variety of goulashes, and there are almost as many ways of making them as there are cooks. This one is the perfect make-ahead dish, as it relies on being stored for a day or two in the refrigerator to develop its rich flavor. You may serve it immediately after it is cooked, if you wish.

Mix flour, salt, and pepper in a paper bag; add the meat cubes and coat well.

In a Dutch oven, heat the oil, and brown the meat. Set the meat aside; add the onions and celery, and cook until they are soft. Add the green peppers, paprika, caraway seeds, the herb bouquet, and the peppercorns. Simmer for 25 minutes, adding water if needed, to prevent mixture from burning. Add the sauerkraut and the broth. Simmer, covered, for 1 1/2 to 2 hours, until the meat is tender. Remove herb bouquet.

Cool, cover, and refrigerate for up to 2 days. To serve, heat over medium heat for about 30 minutes, stirring occasionally. Stir in the sour cream and heat again, without boiling. Serve with spaetzle, homemade noodles (see index), or medium egg noodles.

1/2 cup flour

1 1/2 tsp salt

1/4 to 1/2 tsp pepper

3 1/2 lbs lean pork, cut into 2-inch cubes

1/4 cup oil

3 large onions, chopped

1/2 cup chopped celery

3 green peppers, diced

2 tsp paprika

1/2 tsp caraway seeds

1 Herb Bouquet No. 2 (see index)

4-5 peppercorns

4 cups rinsed, drained, sauerkraut

2 cups beef broth

1/2 cup (or more) sour cream

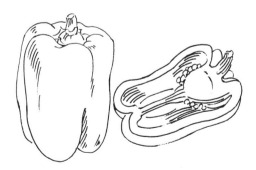

Meats, Poultry and Fish

Meats, Poultry and Fish

Frying Pan Wieners and Sauerkraut

1 serving

1 Tbsp cooking oil

1 cup sauerkraut

¹/₂ medium chopped onion (optional)

2 wieners

Wieners and frankfurters, in all their varieties, have long been used with sauerkraut. This is the simplest way to a delicious hot meal, and the amounts of ingredients may be increased proportionally for a greater number of servings.

Heat the oil in a medium-sized non-stick skillet over medium heat. Add the sauerkraut and fry slowly until the sauerkraut begins to turn golden, adding onion, if wanted. Cut wieners into 1-inch pieces, or leave whole, and fry until they are heated through.

Serve with creamy mashed potatoes and cook some fresh or frozen peas as a side dish.

Wiener Special

4 servings

6 strips bacon, diced

1 onion, sliced

2 cups drained sauerkraut

1 ¹/₂ cups apple juice

1 Tbsp brown sugar

¹/₂ tsp caraway seeds (optional)

2 red-skinned apples

salt and pepper

8-10 wieners

This dish is a more elegant rendition of Frying Pan Wieners and Sauerkraut.

Preheat a large skillet or Dutch oven, and fry the diced bacon until translucent. Add the onion and cook gently, without coloring. Add the sauerkraut, and fry for a few minutes, stirring well. Stir in the apple juice, sugar, and caraway seeds, if using. Grate in one whole apple. Cover and simmer for 45 minutes. Add salt and pepper to taste.

Top with the wieners and simmer for another 20 minutes, or until the wieners are heated through. Core and slice the second apple into rings and garnish the dish with them. Cook for another 10 minutes to soften the apples and heat them through.

Serve with scalloped potatoes and buttered carrots.

Supper Franks and Sauerkraut

6 servings

Frankfurters never tasted so good or looked so nice as in this dish!

In a large skillet, fry the bacon until almost crisp. Drain on paper towels and set aside.

Put the undrained sauerkraut into the pan, adding more fat if needed. Add the water, brown sugar, the instant chicken broth, bay leaves, whole cloves, pepper, and allspice, stirring to mix. Bring to a boil, reduce heat, end simmer for 30 minutes.

Layer the potatoes, tomatoes, and onions on the sauerkraut. Top with whole frankfurters. Simmer for another 20 minutes or more or until the vegetables are soft, and the frankfurters are hot. Garnish with fried bacon.

5 slices bacon, cut into 1-inch pieces

2 cups sauerkraut

¹/₂ cup water

2 Tbsp packed brown sugar

2 envelopes instant chicken broth, undiluted

2-3 bay leaves

3-4 whole cloves

¹/₄ tsp pepper

¹/₄ tsp allspice

3 medium potatoes cut into ¹/₄-inch slices

2 medium tomatoes, cut into ¹/₄-inch slices

2 medium onions, sliced, separated into rings

10-12 frankfurters

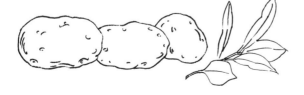

Stuffed Wiener Crown Roast

1 cup onion, chopped

¹/₂ cup diced bacon

4 Tbsp butter or margarine

¹/₂ cup diced celery

1 green pepper, diced

1 apple, pared, diced

2 cups drained, chopped sauerkraut

4 cups slightly dry bread crumbs

¹/₄ tsp caraway seeds

¹/₂ tsp dry mustard

1 tsp oregano

¹/₂ tsp dried thyme

salt and pepper to taste

1 egg, beaten

16 wieners

corn husks (optional)

boiling water

Wieners or frankfurters are not usually considered company fare, but this method of cooking them takes them out of the realm of the ordinary.

In a large skillet, fry the onions and bacon in butter together with the celery and green pepper until soft. Set aside. Add the apple to the pan and cook 1 minute longer. Stir in the sauerkraut with the crumbs and seasonings, adding the onion mixture. Drizzle the egg over the top. Toss lightly to mix well.

Line a deep saucepan, or 6-inch diameter bowl with sufficient foil to cover the sides and bottom, with a 3-inch overhang. Stand the wieners upright around the sides of the pan (they will extend above the top). Spoon the sauerkraut mixture into the centre. If using the corn husks, strip them into ribbons and tie several together to form a rope; otherwise use kitchen string. Tie around the wieners as close as possible to pan's rim. Cover with second foil sheet, crimping the two sheets of foil together.

Lift the foil-wrapped wiener roast into a kettle, and add boiling water to half-way up the package. Maintain the water at a boil about an hour, or until the wiener roast is piping hot, adding water as needed.

When the roast is cooked, lift out of the foil package and set on a serving dish. To serve, spoon out the filling, then pull out wieners with a fork, leaving the string in place.

Variation: Use a Hot Potato Sauerkraut Salad (see index), filling after the wieners are hot.

Pepperoni Supper

4 servings

Sometimes when there is no time to cook a roast or other slower cooking meats, consider preparing a meal with pre-cooked smoked meats.

Preheat oven to 350° F.

In an ovenproof casserole, fry the onion, paprika, and dill until the onions begin to soften. Add ½ cup water, the carrots, and the potatoes. Bring to a boil, and simmer for 10 minutes. Top the vegetables with the sauerkraut, and place the thickly sliced pepperoni on the sauerkraut.

Cover and bake for 20-30 minutes until the vegetables are tender.

Serve with a bowl of sour cream stirred with sufficient mustard to make it tangy.

1 cup chopped onion

paprika to taste

1 Tbsp chopped dill

¹/₂ cup water

2 large carrots, thinly sliced into rounds

2 lbs potatoes, thickly sliced into rounds

2 ¹/₂ cups, drained sauerkraut

1 ¹/₂ lbs pepperoni sausage

sour cream to taste

mustard to taste

Sauerkraut with Kielbasa

4 servings

Kielbasa is a Polish sausage, but you can use any kind you prefer.

In a large skillet, brown the kielbasa in the salad oil. Set aside. Cook the onion, garlic, and peppers in the same frying pan until tender. Add the sauerkraut, water, brown sugar, and the kielbasa. Heat to boiling, then cover and simmer for 15 minutes. Add the apple wedges and cook a few minutes longer.

2 lbs kielbasa cut into 2-inch pieces

4 Tbsp salad oil

1 medium onion, diced

1 clove garlic, minced

1 small hot pepper, minced

1 green pepper, diced

4 cups drained sauerkraut

³/₄ cup water

2 Tbsp brown sugar

1 large red cooking apple, cored, cut in wedges

Garlic Sausage with Sauerkraut

1 medium onion, chopped

¹/₄ cup chopped celery

2 Tbsp bacon fat

2 ¹/₂ cups rinsed, drained sauerkraut

¹/₂ tsp sugar

¹/₄ cup water

1 ¹/₄ lb garlic sausage

salt and pepper to taste

¹/₄ tsp caraway seed (optional)

My mother used to make sausage at home, often for Christmas, or when a pig was being butchered. It is a long time since I have had the opportunity to eat homemade sausage, but the many different sausages available in the grocery stores make good substitutes.

In a large non-stick skillet, fry the onion and celery in the fat until soft. Add the remaining ingredients and sauté slowly over low heat until the sauerkraut begins to brown and is well seasoned with the sausage and the bacon fat.

Fried Sauerkraut with Mushrooms

3 slices salt pork, or bacon, chopped

1 lb lean pork, cubed

1 medium onion, diced

1 cup celery, chopped

water

1 cup sliced mushrooms

2 tomatoes, peeled, diced

4 cups drained sauerkraut

1 lb garlic sausage, sliced into 1-inch rounds

salt and pepper to taste

Other meats may be combined with the sausage.

In a large skillet fry the salt pork or bacon until translucent. Remove fat and reserve. Brown the pork in the drippings. Set aside. Add the onion and celery and cook until soft. Cover the meat with water and simmer until it is almost cooked. Add the mushrooms with the tomatoes and cook for another 10 minutes. Add the sauerkraut, the sliced sausage, and the reserved pork and bacon. Season with salt and pepper to taste. Cover until the sauerkraut is cooked and the flavors are blended.

Variation: This dish may be slightly thickened with browned flour. Brown 3 Tbsp all-purpose flour in 1-2 Tbsp fat. Stir often to assure even browning. Add slowly ¹/₂ cup cold water, stirring vigorously until thickened and smooth. Combine with the sauerkraut.

Pork or Chicken Buttons

4 servings

A tasty luncheon or supper dish, ready in less than an hour.

Dust the pork buttons or chicken nuggets with garlic salt and pepper. In a large non-stick skillet, fry the pork or chicken in 1 Tbsp butter until browned. Remove and set aside. Fry the onions and bacon in the remaining 1 Tbsp butter until they begin to soften. Add the sauerkraut, frying slowly until it begins to brown. Add the cooked meat and stir fry for a few minutes longer until well blended.

1 ¹/₄ lbs pork buttons or chicken nuggets

garlic salt

black pepper to taste

1-2 Tbsp butter

1 medium onion, diced

3 slices bacon, diced

2 ¹/₂ cups drained sauerkraut

Chicken with Beer & Sauerkraut

4-5 servings

Domestic and wild poultry go well with sauerkraut. The following recipe uses beer as the cooking liquid.

Rub the chicken pieces with salt and pepper. In a large skillet, brown in hot oil, a few pieces at a time, and remove to a platter.

Sauté the onion, celery, and bacon until they start to turn color. Add the sauerkraut to the onion mixture, and turn these ingredients into a Dutch oven. Add the beer, carrots, and brown sugar. Top with the chicken pieces. Cover and simmer for 30 minutes. Add the potatoes, and continue simmering another 30 minutes until the chicken is tender, and the vegetables are cooked.

3-lb fryer, cut up

1 tsp salt

pepper to taste

2 Tbsp salad oil

1 large onion, diced

¹/₂ cup celery, diced

¹/₂ cup chopped bacon

4 cups drained sauerkraut

12-oz can beer

4 large carrots, cut in pieces

2 Tbsp brown sugar

4-5 medium potatoes, quartered

Lemon Chicken with Sauerkraut

3-lb roasting chicken

2 tsp olive oil

white pepper to taste

salt to taste

3 cups rinsed, drained sauerkraut

$^1/_4$ tsp ground red pepper

$^1/_2$ tsp rosemary

1 tsp paprika

1 Tbsp chopped parsley

juice of 1 lemon

Lemon chicken is a popular dish, but baking it on a bed of sauerkraut makes it doubly delicious.

Preheat oven to 375° F.

The chicken may be used whole, but it is nicer with the backbone removed. With kitchen or poultry shears, cut up one side of the backbone. Flatten the chicken by spreading it open, skin from vent to neck; press on the breast bone until it cracks, and the chicken stays open. Cut up the other side of the backbone, saving it for stock. Rinse the chicken under cold water, remove the skin and fat. Wipe it with paper towels. Tuck the wing tips under, and put the legs so they point out horizontally.

Brush olive oil on an ovenproof pan large enough to contain the chicken and sauerkraut, and sprinkle it with salt and pepper. Toss the sauerkraut with red pepper, rosemary, paprika, and chopped parsley, and add it to the pan. Rub half the lemon juice over the chicken. Spread the chicken on top of the sauerkraut. Cover.

Bake in the middle of the oven for about 45 minutes. Uncover and rub the rest of the lemon juice into the chicken. If the sauerkraut is browning too quickly, mix it slightly and rearrange it under the chicken. Lower the heat to 350° F and continue cooking for another 45 minutes, or until the chicken begins to brown, but remains moist and tender.

Duck Bake

Tired of the same old duck? Here is a new way to prepare one. It is quite simple to do.

Preheat oven to 350° F.

Wash the duck and remove the fat. Season with salt and pepper. Prick the skin and place in a roaster. Bake until the duck is partially cooked, about 1 hour. Remove from the roaster onto a platter. In the roaster, sauté the bacon and onion until they begin to color. Add the sauerkraut, the savory, and dill together with ½ cup apple juice.

Reduce oven heat to 300° F. Return pan to the oven and bake for 30 minutes, stirring occasionally. Replace the duck on the sauerkraut, add extra apple juice if needed, cover, and continue baking until the duck is tender.

4-5 lb duck, halved

salt and pepper to taste

6 strips bacon, diced

1 large onion, diced

4 cups drained sauerkraut

1 tsp savory

1 tsp dill

½ to 1 cup apple juice

Meats, Poultry and Fish

Wild Duck

1 wild duck

4 slices bacon, diced

1 cup chopped onion

4 cups rinsed sauerkraut, squeezed dry

¹/₂ cup diced celery

2 apples, cored, diced

1-2 Tbsp chopped parsley

¹/₂ tsp grated orange peel

1 cup ginger ale

2 slices bacon

Wild duck is a treat, but when it comes from a marshy area, it will probably have an unpleasant, fishy taste. This recipe provides directions for eliminating that fishiness.

To remove the duck's wild flavor, soak the plucked, gutted bird for at least 4 hours, or overnight. To make the soaking solution: to each quart of water, add 2 Tbsp salt and 2 tsp baking soda. After soaking the duck, rinse in fresh water and wipe dry.

Preheat oven to 325° F.

In a medium-sized skillet, fry together the bacon with the onions until both begin to change color.

Place the sauerkraut in a large bowl. Add the onion, bacon, celery, diced apples, and parsley. Stuff the duck's cavity, truss it. Prick the skin with a fork several times. Place in a roasting pan and place the remaining two strips of bacon on the duck's breast. Cover and bake for 1 ¹/₂ hours. Remove any fat in the roaster. Mix the orange peel with the ginger ale, and baste the duck with it. Continue to bake for another hour, basting the duck frequently

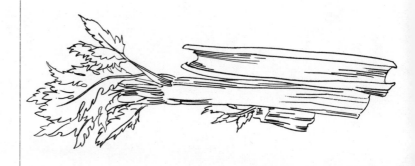

Duck with Oranges and Grapes

4 servings

Here is an adaptation of an unusual dish which originated in German kitchens.

Mix the flour, salt, pepper, and savory. Dredge the duck with the flour mixture, and brown on all sides in the bacon fat or oil in a large skillet. Sauté the diced bacon and onion in the remaining fat.

Preheat oven to 350° F.

Mix the sauerkraut with the bacon, onion, and sugar, and put into a casserole. Arrange the duck quarters on top, and add the mandarin oranges, grapes, wine, and broth. Bake uncovered for 1 hour or more, or until the duck is tender.

¹/₂ cup flour

salt and pepper

¹/₂ tsp savory

4 to 5-lb duck, quartered

2 Tbsp bacon fat or cooking oil

4 cups rinsed sauerkraut, squeezed dry

3 strips bacon, diced

1 large onion, diced

1 tsp sugar

1 cup mandarin oranges, drained

1 cup seedless grapes

¹/₂ cup white wine

1 cup chicken broth

Bohemian Roast Goose

10-lb goose

salt and pepper to taste

1 Tbsp goose fat

1 cup diced celery

1 large onion, diced

1 large apple, cored, diced

6 cups rinsed sauerkraut, squeezed dry

1 tsp caraway seed

1 Tbsp dried dill

$^1/_2$ cup dry wine

2 potatoes, peeled, grated

2-3 Tbsp flour

1 cup water or stock

Goose is wonderful for Christmas and other festive occasions, especially when accompanied by a sauerkraut stuffing.

Wash the goose thoroughly. Dry well and remove as much fat as possible. Prick the skin with a fork under the wings. Salt and pepper the inside.

Make the stuffing by melting the goose fat in a skillet. Sauté the celery, onion, and apple together until they soften. Add the sauerkraut, season with salt and pepper to taste; add the caraway seeds, the dill. Sauté for about 10 minutes. Add the wine and bring to a slow boil. Gradually add the grated potatoes, stirring between additions. Cook slowly, uncovered, until the mixture is fairly thick and dry. Stuff the goose when the dressing is cool enough to handle.

Preheat the oven to 425° F.

Put the goose, trussed or skewered, into a large roasting pan. Cover and place in the oven. Immediately turn down the heat to 300°-325° F.

When the goose is tender, in about 3-4 hours, remove from the roasting pan to a cutting board. Untruss, remove the dressing, and slice or spoon it onto a large, heated platter. Carve the goose and put the slices on top of the dressing.

Drain all but 2 Tbsp fat from the roasting pan, and set pan on a stovetop burner over moderate heat. Mix 2-3 Tbsp flour with a little water in a small bowl and make a smooth paste. Gradually add the remaining water or stock to the paste. Stir into the boiling fat, stirring until the gravy is smooth and thick.

Variations:
- This stuffing is also good to use with a turkey. Use the same amount per pound of turkey as for goose.
- You can stuff a duck by using half this amount.

Thanksgiving Goose

10-12 servings

Preheat oven to 375° F.

Wash goose inside and out. Blot dry, and remove as much fat as possible. Remove giblets and reserve for gravy (recipe follows). Salt the inside of the goose.

Put the sauerkraut into a bowl with the carrots and apples. In a skillet, melt the butter, add the celery, onion, and bacon, and cook until just turning color. Add to the sauerkraut and mix well. Season to taste. Fit a stuffing bag into the goose's cavity and fill. Close the vent.

Place the goose in a roasting pan. Rub the skin with lemon juice. Prick the skin under the wings and the legs. Place the salt pork across the breast. Roast uncovered for 45 minutes. Drain the fat from the pan and pour the apple juice or cider around the goose. Cover. Reduce oven heat to 300° F; replace goose in the oven, and continue cooking for 4-5 hours, allowing 30 minutes per pound, or until tender.

10-12 lb goose

salt and pepper

4 cups rinsed sauerkraut, squeezed dry

2 ½ cups grated carrots

2 apples, cored, chopped

2 Tbsp butter

1 cup celery, diced

1 large onion, diced

4 strips bacon, diced

juice of 1 lemon

6 strips salt pork

1 cup apple juice or apple cider

Thanksgiving Gravy

Put the giblets in a saucepan and cover with water. Add the vegetables, salt and pepper, and simmer for 35-45 minutes. Remove the giblets and drain the stock into another pan. Bring to a boil.

In a medium-sized pan, brown the flour in the butter or goose fat. Gradually add the hot stock, stirring to make a smooth paste. Stir into the remaining stock, heat gradually until gravy thickens. If a few lumps remain in the gravy, strain it. Correct the seasonings before serving.

goose giblets

water

2 carrots

½ cup celery leaves

1 onion, quartered

1 parsnip

2-3 Tbsp flour

3 Tbsp butter or goose fat

salt and pepper

Stuffed Goose

8-lb goose

4 cups partially drained sauerkraut

1 onion, chopped

2 potatoes, grated

1 cup cooked rice

salt and pepper to taste

This simple way of stuffing a goose is for those who love the tartness of sauerkraut.

Preheat oven to 400° F.

Wash the goose; remove as much fat as possible. Prick under the wings and legs. Put into a roaster, uncovered, and bake for 30-40 minutes. Remove from oven, and drain off the fat.

Simmer the sauerkraut with the onion for 30 minutes. Add grated potatoes gradually, stirring until the sauerkraut is very thick. Add the cooked rice. Season with salt and pepper to taste. Mix well, and cool. Stuff and skewer goose. Reduce oven temperature to 300° F. Continue baking the goose until tender, about 3-4 hours.

Game Birds in Sauerkraut

1 Tbsp cooking oil

2 Tbsp butter

2 game birds, trussed

1 ½ lbs chorizo, Hungarian salami, or 4 sweet Italian sausage

medium onions, diced

3 cloves garlic, minced

2 apples, cored, chopped

½ cup diced bacon

3 cups drained sauerkraut

2 or more cups white wine

Slow cooking tenderizes meat. Here, game birds— grouse, duck, or partridge—are combined with sausage, wine and apple juice. If you like a spicy version, use a hot chorizo sausage.

Preheat the oven to 325° F.

In a large Dutch oven, heat oil and butter. Brown the trussed birds on all sides and remove from the pot. Brown the sausage lightly, then remove from the pot. Sauté the onion, garlic, chopped apple, and bacon in the remaining fat until they become limp. Add the sauerkraut and stir well; place the birds breast side down in the sauerkraut, and bury the sausage in the sauerkraut beside them.

Bake for 1 ½ hours or until the birds are tender, adding more wine if necessary.

Holubtsi

Holubtski, or "little pigeons" in Ukrainian, are cabbage rolls, and are considered a part of their national cuisine by many Slavic people. Their popularity has spread because they are so delicious, and cabbage rolls are now popular in a great many countries. Recipes are numerous, and everybody has a favorite way of making them. Here, holubtsi are made with sauerkraut, and I have provided for a number of fillings. First, the basic recipe.

Ukrainian-Style Cabbage Rolls

(Holubtsi)

Old-fashioned holubtsi, or cabbage rolls made from heads of cabbage cured in sauerkraut, are delicious and enjoyable fare. Some may find cabbage rolls made solely from these cured cabbage heads too strongly flavored for their taste. A less pungent taste can be obtained by making half the rolls from fresh cabbage, and alternating the layers in the casserole.

The method of making cabbage rolls is the same whether you use fresh cabbage or one cured in sauerkraut. Remove as much of the core as possible. Separate the leaves, one by one, taking care not tear them. If the leaves of the cured cabbage are very sour, soak them briefly in warm water. Fresh cabbage leaves are put in very hot water and allowed to soften. Remove the center rib from each leaf. Cut the large leaves into 3-4 sections.

Prepare the rice filling—or any favorite filling of cereal, including kasha, which is popular—or combinations of cereal and meat, western favorites. Refer to Fillings (see index).

Ukrainian-Style Cabbage Rolls

2 cups washed rice

2 tsp salt

2 cups boiling water

1 onion, finely chopped

¼ cup or more diced bacon

3-4 Tbsp butter or oil, or a combination

Rice Filling

The filling should be well-seasoned, as some of the seasoning will be absorbed by the leaves.

Add rice and salt to boiling water, return to a brisk boil for 1 minute. Turn off the heat, and allow rice to stand until the water is absorbed. The rice will be partially cooked.

In a medium-sized skillet, fry the onion and bacon in butter, oil, or a combination of both, until it is golden. Mix with the rice and season to taste.

Put a generous spoonful of filling on each leaf, roll snugly, turning the leaf sides over the filling, if necessary. If you have softened the cabbage and make the rolls reasonably small, toothpicks are not required to hold them together. Prepare a large pot by generously lining it with cabbage leaves and/or bacon rind. Layer the cabbage rolls, seam side down in the pot and add one of the following cooking sauces:

1 ½ cups tomato juice

½ cup sour cream

salt and pepper to taste

2 Tbsp or more butter or bacon fat

Tomato-Sour Cream

Combine the ingredients, adding the tomato juice slowly to the sour cream, stirring constantly to make it smooth. Pour over the holubtsi. The liquid should show just between the rolls.

Tomato Soup

Thin a 10-oz can of condensed tomato soup with a 10-oz can of water.

Soup Stock

Use a soup stock, either chicken, beef, or pork.

Ukrainian-Style Cabbage Rolls *(continued)*

Mushroom Stock

Use liquid from canned mushrooms or soak several dried mushrooms in 2 cups of water. Put all ingredients in a small saucepan, cover, and simmer for 45 minutes. Strain, reserving liquid and discarding the vegetables. Add enough chicken stock or canned consommé to make 6 cups.

1 lb mushrooms, chopped

1 small carrot, halved

1 small onion, halved

1-2 stalks celery, cut in large pieces

3-4 cups water, chicken stock, or canned consommé

Tomato Paste

Use a 6-oz can, or more, of tomato paste diluted with water. Season with salt and pepper.

Tomato Juice

Cover the holubtsi and the tomato juice with a few more cabbage leaves. Cover tightly, and bake in a 300° F oven for 1 1/2 to 2 hours, or until the cabbage and filling is cooked. Serve the holubtsi with dressings of

- fried crisp bacon and dripping
- diced onion and diced bacon fried in lard, oil, butter, or a combination of 1 tsp oil and 2 Tbsp butter (you get the butter flavor and no burnt butter)
- sour cream
- tomato sauce

Smetana Sauce With Green Onions

Bring cream to the boil. Add onion, dill, and season with salt and pepper. Simmer very slowly until flavors are blended and sauce is thickened.

2 cups sour cream or thick sweet cream

1/2 cup or more chopped green onions

salt and pepper

2 tsp chopped dill (optional)

(continued)

Ukrainian-Style Cabbage Rolls

Alternative Cooking Methods

At Christmas, or other times when the oven will be too full of other dishes, large quantities of *holubtsi* can be cooked overnight in a 200° to 225° F oven. Put them in late in the evening and check early in the morning, or they will overcook. Reheat before serving.

Holubtsi may also be cooked in a pressure cooker for 10 minutes at 10 lbs pressure.

Sauerkraut *Holubtsi No. 2*

Sometimes it is difficult to find pickled heads of cabbage but you can still have sauerkraut holubtsi by following this recipe.

Follow the directions for Ukrainian-Style Cabbage Rolls (see index), but use fresh cabbage leaves. Sprinkle each layer with some shredded sauerkraut. The cabbage rolls will not require extra salt, although some of the brine may be used as part of the cooking liquid for extra flavor. These holubtsi will have a nice delicate flavor of sauerkraut.

Pork and Sauerkraut Rolls

6 servings

Make the filling by putting the sausage meat in a large bowl. Add the onion, rice, garlic salt, dry mustard, savory, salt and pepper to taste. Mix well.

Prepare a large casserole or Dutch oven by covering the bottom with a few large leaves of cabbage. Top with 1 cup of sauerkraut.

Soften the cabbage leaves by putting them into very hot water for a few minutes. Cut out the centre rib and halve the leaves, or quarter them if they are very large.

Put a spoonful of filling on each leaf and roll it up. Lay the cabbage rolls seam side down on the sauerkraut. After all the rolls are in place, cover with the remaining sauerkraut. Put the pork hock on top. Add water to partially cover, and bring to a boil. Immediately reduce heat, and cook, covered, on top of the stove.

Alternatively, bake in a 300° F oven for 2-3 hours, adding more water if necessary.

When serving, top with a spoonful or two of sour cream and sprinkle with paprika.

1/2 lb bulk pork sausage meat

1/2 cup minced onion

2 cups partially cooked rice

1/2 tsp garlic salt

1/2 tsp dry mustard

1/2 tsp savory

salt and pepper to taste

8-10 large cabbage leaves

2 cups drained sauerkraut

1 smoked pork hock

2 cups sour cream

paprika to taste

3-Meat Sauerkraut Rolls

³/₄ cup washed rice

1 ¹/₂ cups boiling water

8 slices bacon, diced

6 medium onions, chopped

1 ¹/₄ lb lean pork, minced

2 eggs

¹/₂ tsp dry mustard

¹/₂ tsp celery salt

¹/₂ tsp savory

1 tsp garlic powder

salt and paprika to taste

1-2 heads sauerkraut

6-7 veal cutlets

2 Tbsp bacon fat

bacon rind or slices

1 lb smoked meat, sliced

³/₄ lb Hungarian salami or any firm sausage

Hungarians prepare a special recipe, a cabbage roll dish for company, which is time-consuming, but the results are well worthwhile. Here is a version of that dish.

In a small saucepan, cook the rice in boiling water for 8-10 minutes. Drain if necessary; then put into a large bowl.

Using a small non-stick skillet, fry the bacon and onion until wilted. Add to the rice. Add the pork, eggs, dry mustard, celery salt, savory, and garlic powder. Season with salt and paprika to taste.

Core the cured cabbage heads and separate the leaves. Remove the centre rib from the leaves, and halve each leaf. Place a spoonful of the filling on each piece of leaf, and roll it, tucking in the edges if needed.

Line a large casserole or Dutch oven with larger cabbage leaves, bacon rind, or a few thick slices of bacon.

Preheat oven to 325°-350° F.

In a large skillet, fry the cutlets in bacon fat for a few minutes to brown each side. Place the smoked meat slices in the casserole or Dutch oven. Chop the unused portion of the pickled cabbage heads after you have made the rolls. If all the leaves are used, you can use some sauerkraut. Put the shredded sauerkraut on top of the smoked meat, then the rolls tucked side by side. Put in the veal cutlets next, and top with the sausage slices. Sprinkle each layer with paprika.

Bake for about 3 hours or until the meat and the rolls are tender.

Traditionally, this dish is made four days ahead and is warmed and cooled on three days, and served on the fourth. It is claimed that this process blends the flavors together, but I have never tested this tradition.

New Year's Sauerkraut

(Kapama po Banski)

This festive dish originates in the mountains of Bulgaria. It is made for special occasions such as weddings, New Year's Eve parties, or important family gatherings. It features chicken or rabbit, pork, and blood sausage arranged on a large platter and surrounded with sauerkraut rolls.

In a large skillet, fry the onion together with the garlic and pork sausage meat, using part of the fat. Stir in the rice, salt, pepper, and sage; mix well and add 1 cup water. Simmer gently until the rice and meat are cooked, about 20 minutes.

Core the cabbages and separate the leaves. Remove part of the rib from each leaf, and halve or quarter larger leaves. Place a spoonful of the meat-rice filling on each leaf and roll tightly, tucking in the sides if necessary. Chop up any unused parts of the sauerkraut heads, reserving several of the larger leaves.

Wash the chicken or rabbit, and stuff the cavity with unused rice and meat mixture.

Preheat oven to 325-350° F.

Line a large oven-proof cooking pot with bacon rind and larger pieces of streaky bacon. Top with a layer of chopped sauerkraut-heads or sauerkraut, then the chicken or rabbit, and the spare ribs or pork bones. Place the sauerkraut rolls over and between them. Sprinkle generously with pepper. Place the whole blood sausage on top. Cover with several layers of cabbage leaves. Pour in 1 cup of water and seal tightly with a lid and aluminium foil.

Bring cooking pot to a boil over medium heat, and place immediately into oven. Cook slowly for 3 or more hours, until the chicken, or rabbit, and the cabbage rolls are well cooked and tender.

To serve, place the chicken and blood sausage in the middle of a large platter, and arrange around the cabbage rolls and the sauerkraut with the bacon pieces.

3 medium onions, diced

1 clove garlic, minced

2 1/2 lbs pork sausage meat

1/4 cup fat

1 cup washed rice

salt to taste

2 tsp pepper

1 tsp sage

2 cups water

2 large heads sauerkraut

1 large chicken or rabbit

bacon rind

2 lbs streaky bacon, cut in pieces

1 lb meaty pork bones or spareribs

1 whole blood sausage

New Year's Savories

1 ¹/2 lbs veal, minced

1 lb pork sausage meat

1 onion, finely chopped

1 Tbsp parsley, minced

¹/2 cup rice, parboiled

2 Tbsp tomato paste

2 cloves garlic, minced

pepper and paprika

1 tsp salt

10 slices bacon

bacon rind (optional)

sauerkraut leaves

¹/2 cup cold water

¹/2 cup sauerkraut juice

Bulgaria's New Year includes these tasty tidbits which are served with the celebratory supper. They also make interesting appetizers for other occasions.

Mix the meats with onion, parsley, rice, tomato paste, garlic, pepper, paprika to taste, and salt. Set aside.

In a non-stick skillet, fry the bacon slices until translucent. Prepare a casserole or Dutch oven by placing the bacon rind on the bottom and a few cabbage leaves over it. Arrange the bacon slices over the top.

Preheat oven to 350° F.

Make the rolls by cutting the sauerkraut leaves into pieces 2 ¹/2 inches by 2 ¹/2 inches, removing any hard ribs. Place a small spoonful of prepared meat filling on each square, then roll tightly or make a small package. Place them side by side, seam side down, on top of the bacon slices. Cover with more leaves.

Pour in the water and sauerkraut juice. Cover and bake for 1 hour or until very tender.

Linyvi Holubtsi (Lazy Rolls)

4-6 servings

For cooks too swamped with work to make cabbage rolls, here is a recipe that provides a good, flavorful supper dish. Make this dish ahead and cook it when needed.

Combine the rice, water, salt, and 1 Tbsp butter. Cover tightly, reduce the heat, and simmer for about 8-10 minutes. Shut off the heat and let stand, tightly covered, for another 10-15 minutes. The rice should be fluffy and cooked.

In a large skillet, fry the diced bacon and onion until translucent. Add the dillweed, the sauerkraut, and ¹/₂ cup tomato juice, and cook for about 15 minutes, stirring occasionally. Season to taste.

Preheat oven to 350° F.

Butter an ample baking dish and layer the sauerkraut mixture and rice. Repeat layers ending with the sauerkraut. Pour in the remaining tomato juice until level with the top layer.

Top with bread crumbs, or if you prefer, strips of bacon. Cover and bake for about an hour, until the flavors are well blended.

Variations:
- Add ¹/₂ cup chopped ham to the rice.
- Add 1 cupful of chopped mushrooms to the sauerkraut.
- Add 1 cup chopped, cooked chicken to the rice.
- Sweet or sour cream may be used as part of the liquid.

1 ¹/₂ cups washed rice

2 ¹/₂ cups boiling water

1 tsp salt

1 Tbsp butter

¹/₂ cup bacon, diced

1 medium onion, diced

1 Tbsp chopped dillweed

2 ¹/₂ cups partially drained sauerkraut

1 ³/₄ cup tomato juice

salt and pepper to taste

2 Tbsp butter

¹/₂ cup buttered crumbs (optional)

4-5 strips bacon (optional)

Fish

Fish and sauerkraut complement each other, as these recipes from Central Europe demonstrate. Sauerkraut can absorb a lot of fat which seems to make it more flavorful. North American cooks may not wish to use as much fat as the Europeans who created these recipes. I am not fond of using excessive amounts of cooking fats and have halved the amounts without spoiling the dishes.

The fish used in the original recipes are not always available in North America, so I use what I have on hand, or purchase fish which seem close in texture and flavor. These substitutions may change the flavor of the dish, but not necessarily for the worse! Experiment to obtain the best results.

Bulgarian Fish Fillets

4-6 servings

1 onion, diced

1 clove garlic, minced

4 strips bacon, diced

1/2 cup cooking oil

4 cups sauerkraut, partially drained

1/4 cup bread crumbs

2 lbs white, firm-fleshed fish fillets

salt and pepper to taste

1/2 tsp paprika

In Bulgaria, this simple dish of sauerkraut and fish is easy to put together and is baked only long enough for the fish to be cooked.

Preheat oven to 350° F.

Using a medium-sized skillet, fry the onion, garlic, and bacon in 2 Tbsp oil until lightly colored. Place the sauerkraut in a bowl, and add the onion, garlic, and bacon.

Grease a baking dish and line with the sauerkraut mixture. Sprinkle with bread crumbs. Season the fish fillets with the salt, pepper, and the paprika; place them on top of the sauerkraut. Pour over the remaining oil. Bake for 30-35 minutes, or until the fish flakes easily.

Catfish and Sauerkraut

4-6 servings

This Bulgarian recipe uses catfish, unavailable in many regions. Any mild-flavored fish can be substituted.

Using a small skillet, fry the bacon and onion in 2 Tbsp oil until they start to become translucent. Put the sauerkraut into a large pot; add the bacon, onion, and the herb bouquet with the garlic. Simmer for 35-45 minutes. Drain and discard the herb bouquet and garlic.

Mix flour into the remaining oil and heat. Season with paprika, salt, and pepper. Let the mixture begin to brown, then add it to the sauerkraut. Stir until it thickens, but is not too thick. Cut the fish into pieces. Add them to the sauerkraut. Bring to a boil, lower the heat, and simmer for 20-30 minutes, until the fish is cooked. Pour in the sour cream and continue to heat, but do not allow to boil.

^{1}/$_2$ cup diced bacon

1 onion, diced

^{1}/$_2$ cup cooking oil

4 cups drained sauerkraut

1 Herb Bouquet No. 6 (see index)

1 clove garlic

2-3 Tbsp flour

paprika

salt and pepper to taste

2 lbs catfish

1 cup sour cream

Fish and Wine Casserole

4-6 servings

Wine with fish and sauerkraut is just as good as wine with other meats. This Romanian recipe calls for carp which is not generally available in North America, so substitute another mild-flavored fish.

Preheat oven to 325° F.

Cut the fish in serving size pieces and salt them. Fry the onion and bacon in a small skillet until they begin to soften, and add the sauerkraut. Mix well. Put the sauerkraut into a baking dish, top with tomato slices and fish. Add the bay leaves, peppercorns, and cloves. Mix the wine and oil and pour over all. Bake for about 45 minutes or until the fish is cooked.

3 lbs carp

salt to taste

1 onion, diced

3 strips bacon, diced

4 cups drained sauerkraut

3 tomatoes, peeled, sliced

3 bay leaves

6-8 peppercorns

3 whole cloves

^{1}/$_2$ cup white wine

^{1}/$_2$ cup oil

Sauerkraut with Fish, Russian-Style

6 servings

1 large onion, diced

6 Tbsp margarine or butter

3 cups drained sauerkraut

1-2 Tbsp vinegar

1 tsp basil

salt and pepper to taste

water

1 ½ lbs white, firm-fleshed fish, sliced 1 ½ inches thick

1 large dill pickle, sliced

20-oz can mushrooms, stems and pieces

½ cup sliced black olives

The Russians have created many fish recipes, including this unusual one which uses olives, pickles, and mushrooms. The combination is great!

In a large skillet, sauté the onion in 4 Tbsp margarine or butter until soft. Add the drained sauerkraut, vinegar, basil, salt and pepper to taste. Sauté for a couple of minutes to blend well.

Preheat oven to 350° F.

Cook the fish in a small amount of water, 2 minutes a side, cool, and break into pieces, discarding as much bone as possible. Line a 2-quart casserole with half the sauerkraut mixture and all the fish. Sprinkle with half the sliced dill pickle, mushrooms, and sliced olives. Cover with the sauerkraut and repeat the layers of pickle, mushrooms, and olives. Dot with remaining margarine or butter.

Cover the casserole and bake for 35-45 minutes.

German Fish Pudding

6-8 servings

This traditional dish, Hechtenkraut oder Fisch-pudding mit Sauerkraut, was served to royalty a couple of centuries ago. It remains a tasty dish and can be prepared by anybody who has the time.

In a medium-sized skillet, fry the bacon and onion in butter until slightly colored. Put the sauerkraut into a large pan or Dutch oven. Add the onion and bacon together with the peppercorns, garlic salt, sugar, and caraway seeds. Pour in 1 cup of wine or apple cider, and add enough stock to reach halfway up the sauerkraut. Simmer slowly for 1 ½ hours until the sauerkraut is tender but not too soft. In the last half hour of cooking add the grated potato, stirring until very thick, adding an extra dash of wine at the last minute for flavor.

3 strips bacon, diced

½ cup minced onion

3 Tbsp butter

4 cups drained sauerkraut

6 peppercorns

½ tsp garlic salt

2 tsp sugar

1 tsp caraway seeds (optional)

¾ to 1 cup white wine, or apple cider

vegetable or fish soup stock

1 large potato, grated

The Pudding

Cook the fish in stock or water along with 1 onion, celery, carrot, herb bouquet, and salt. When the fish is cooked, strain and reserve the stock.

Preheat oven to 375° F.

In a small skillet, fry the bacon until it begins to melt, add 2 onions, and continue frying until the onions begin to change color.

Butter a large baking dish. Sprinkle with bread crumbs, covering sides and bottom. Place a layer of the prepared sauerkraut mixture on the bottom; sprinkle with the bacon and onion mixture. Then put in some fish. Repeat the layers, ending with the sauerkraut.

Pour the sauce over the fish pudding. Top with buttered crumbs. Bake for 35-45 minutes until the topping is browned.

2 ½ lbs white, firm-fleshed fish

stock or water

3 onions, minced

3 stalks celery, diced

1 large carrot, diced

1 Herb Bouquet No. 3 (see index)

salt and pepper to taste

¾ cup diced bacon

3-4 Tbsp butter

bread crumbs

sauerkraut

buttered bread crumbs

(continued)

German Fish Pudding

2 Tbsp butter

3-4 Tbsp flour

¹/₂ cup sweet cream

stock

salt and pepper to taste

1 tsp paprika

Sauce

Melt 2 Tbsp butter in a skillet and add the flour, stirring over low heat until the flour is a light golden brown, about 5-6 minutes.

Remove from heat, and add the cream, stirring vigorously to prevent lumping. Add more stock as needed to make a thick, smooth sauce.

Season with salt, pepper, and paprika. Cook until the sauce begins to bubble.

Variations:
- Thickly slice some boiled potatoes and carrots and add just before putting in the oven.
- You can fry the fish instead. Dip the fish in beaten eggs and dredge in bread crumbs. Quickly brown in hot butter or other fat.

Pastas with Sauerkraut

Pastas with Sauerkraut

Pasta goes well with all meats and vegetables. It can be combined in many ways. Homemade noodles, in my opinion, are the tastiest, but there are a great many commercial varieties that are suitable for any of these dishes.

Poppy Seed Noodle Bake

6-8 servings

¹/₂ cups uncooked linguine

¹/₂ tsp salt

1 ¹/₂ lbs pork sausage links

1 cup sour cream

¹/₂ cup cottage cheese

2 Tbsp melted butter

1 ¹/₂ Tbsp poppy seed

1 tsp onion salt

¹/₂ tsp pepper

3 cups drained sauerkraut

¹/₂ cup milk (optional)

Here is a pasta combined with pork sausages and sauerkraut. The surprise ingredients are poppy seeds and cottage cheese. The dish is rich with sour cream.

Cook the linguine to al dente in boiling water with the ¹/₂ tsp salt. Drain and set aside.

Put the pork sausages in a pot of warm water. Bring to a boil, reduce heat, and simmer for 6-8 minutes. Drain well.

Preheat oven to 350° F.

Combine the sour cream, cottage cheese, melted butter, poppy seeds, salt and pepper with the noodles and the sauerkraut. If the result is too thick, add some milk to thin it. Put into a 4-qt baking dish.

In a non-stick skillet, brown the sausages slightly, turning them often for an even color. Arrange these in a pinwheel fashion on top of the sauerkraut and noodle mixture. Bake for 35-40 minutes. Serve with a tossed salad.

Sauerkraut and Noodles

6 servings

If you don't care for sour cream, or don't happen to have any on hand, try this version of sauerkraut and noodles.

Preheat oven to 350° F.

Cook the noodles in boiling, salted water until al dente. Drain, butter, and set aside.

Into a non-stick skillet, put bacon and the onion; fry until wilted. Add the sauerkraut and fry gently until it begins to change color.

Butter a casserole dish and layer the sauerkraut and buttered noodles. Repeat layers, ending with sauerkraut. Pour tomato juice over deep enough to reach the top layer. Bake for 30-35 minutes until the flavors are well blended. Serve hot.

2 1/2 cups uncooked linguine

1-2 Tbsps butter or margarine

1/2 cup diced bacon

1 cup diced onion

3 cups drained sauerkraut

1-2 cups tomato juice

Hamburger Noodle Casserole

1 8-oz pkg egg noodles

3 cups drained sauerkraut

1 medium onion, chopped

2 Tbsp butter or margarine

1 ¹/₂ lbs lean ground beef

1 egg

1 cup soft bread crumbs

1 tsp salt

¹/₄ to ¹/₂ tsp pepper

1 tsp dry mustard

¹/₂ tsp savory

¹/₈ tsp ground thyme

1 clove garlic, crushed

¹/₃ cup milk

2 to 2 ¹/₂ cups stewed tomatoes

This version of a noodle bake makes use of ground beef, making a complete dish suitable for lunch or a light supper. It is German-style cuisine.

Preheat oven to 350° F.

Cook the noodles in salted water until al dente. Drain. Put in a large bowl and stir in the sauerkraut. In a medium-sized skillet, fry the onion lightly in 1 Tbsp butter, and stir gently into the noodles and sauerkraut.

Blend together the ground beef with the eggs, bread crumbs, salt, and other spices, crushed garlic, and milk. Shape into small balls. Brown them in the remaining butter or margarine; stir in the tomatoes, chopping them into pieces if they are whole. Using a large, covered casserole dish, spoon in half of the noodle mixture, followed by the meat balls and tomatoes. Repeat layers. Cover. Bake about 45 minutes, until bubbly in the centre.

Swabian Sauerkraut & Homemade Noodles

6-8 servings

Here is an excellent example of how well pasta goes with sauerkraut. This German recipe is served with easily prepared homemade noodles, but you could use Spaetzle, Egg Drop Dumplings (see index), or a pound of commercial egg noodles.

Heat the butter or lard in a large skillet, adding the onion and garlic, and sautéing slowly until they soften. Add the sauerkraut and cook slowly over low heat until it begins to turn golden.

Precook the back bacon or spare ribs in a small amount of water, or braise in a pan until they are tender. Add the chopped ham or pork loin to the sauerkraut mixture. Season.

4 Tbsp butter or lard

1 onion, minced

2 cloves garlic, minced

5 cups, rinsed, drained sauerkraut

1 lb back bacon or spareribs, cut in small pieces

1 lb cooked ham or pork loin, diced

salt and pepper to taste

homemade noodles (recipe follows) or spaetzle

Homemade Noodles

1 egg

2 Tbsp water

dash of salt

1 to 1 ¼ cups flour

Homemade Noodles are made with similar ingredients to those used in Egg Drop Dumplings and Spaetzle. They are time-consuming to make, but they are superior to any commercial dry noodles. You can use them in place of Spaetzle or Egg Drop Dumplings.

Beat the egg with water and a dash of salt. Sift flour in a bowl and make a depression in the centre. Pour in the beaten egg-water mixture and gradually work into the flour until the dough holds together. Add a little flour if the dough appears to be sticky. Turn dough onto a pastry board, and continue mixing and kneading until it is smooth and elastic. Shape into a ball, dust with flour, and let stand for 15-20 minutes. Cut the dough into thirds and roll each third to tissue thinness. Place rolled-out dough onto a clean cloth and let dry for 20 minutes.

Roll each piece of dough jelly roll-wise; then, with a sharp knife, cut across the roll to make noodles of the width required—⅛ to ¼-inch for soups, or up to 1 inch for other dishes. Scatter the noodles on a clean cloth to dry for approximately 5-6 hours.

Dried noodles can keep for weeks in a tightly covered jar or sealed in plastic bags and frozen.

To cook, boil in salted water for 8-10 minutes; drain and rinse quickly in cold water. Add to the sauerkraut and mix in well before serving.

The noodles may be added to chicken or beef broth before serving, or buttered and served with stews and goulash.

Kraut and Homemade Noodles

4-5 servings

This recipe makes use of Homemade Noodles in a very simple way. It is quick to do and can be varied by adding bacon and onions to the sauerkraut.

Knead the dough until it is the consistency of bread dough—soft, but not sticky. Roll into a rectangle 1-inch thick. Cut into pieces 1-inch long by 1-inch wide, and cook in boiling, salted water until very little water is left. Drain.

Fry the sauerkraut in oil until just colored. Add the dumplings, mix well, and cook for a few minutes longer.

1 recipe Homemade Noodles dough (see previous recipe)

boiling water

$1/2$ tsp salt

1-2 Tbsp cooking oil

4 cups drained sauerkraut

Kraut Dumplings

4-5 servings

Knead the dough until it has the consistency of bread dough—soft, but not sticky. Roll into a rectangle 1 inch thick. Cut into pieces 1-inch by 1-inch square, and cook in salted boiling water until there is very little water left.

In a medium-sized skillet, fry the sauerkraut in the oil until just colored. Add the dumplings, mix well, and cook for a few minutes longer.

1 recipe Homemade Noodles Dough (see previous recipes)

boiling water

$1/2$ tsp salt

1-2 Tbsp cooking oil

4 cups drained sauerkraut

Perogies or Stuffed Dumplings

Perogies, perohy, vareniky, pelemeni, kolduny, uszka, calsones, and monti are stuffed dumplings from Poland, the Ukraine, Russia, Italy, and the Far East. The names vary with the country, as do the shapes, and filling, but they are all made from a similar dough. Thus, it is traditional to fill kolduny with meat, and to make them in a rounded shape; the Russian pelemeni are folded into half moon shapes, filled with meats, and are eaten with soy sauce, mustard, butter, and vinegar. They are said to be descendants of the dim sum pastries of China. Central Russian versions are curled and pinched to resemble shells; they are eaten with sour cream, butter, mustard, or a broth.

Filled dumplings have become popular in Canada in the past decade or so, and they can now be purchased in most grocery stores under the Polish name perogies. Canadians usually eat them dressed with fried onion and bacon or ham, and serve them with sour cream. They are usually either triangular or shaped into half moons.

Although store-bought perogies are good, these delicious morsels may be made at home. There are numerous ways of making dough for filled dumplings and, as one can expect, each country has some variation of its own. All are good, and eventually a cook will find his/her own favorite. The dough should be medium soft and smooth, but not sticky. Experience is the best teacher. Make them often enough and you will soon be able to tell if the dough is just right. Even a dough that is not quite right will still make edible perogies. It is very difficult to give the number of perogies you can make from a batch of dough. The amounts given are based on squares approximately 2 inches by 2 inches.

The Traditional Dough

about 48

Sift together the flour and salt. With a fork, beat the egg with some of the water and all the oil or fat. Make a well in the flour. Add the egg mixture to the flour. Mix and knead, adding enough water to make a medium soft dough. Knead until the dough is smooth and elastic. Put in a bowl and cover well with a cloth or piece of plastic. Let the dough rest for about 30 minutes, or the dough will shrink as it is rolled.

4 1/2 cups flour

1 tsp salt

1 egg

water

3 Tbsp cooking oil or melted shortening

Potato-Water Dough

between 35-50 pieces

Sift the flour with the salt. Mix oil and water. Pour into the flour and keep kneading until the dough is smooth and elastic, adding more water if required. Cover and let rest 30 minutes before rolling.

2 tsp salt

5 cups flour

1/4 cup cooking oil

2 cups very hot potato water (cook potatoes, use drained water for liquid, and add water to make up any shortage)

Sour Cream Dough

about 30 pieces

Sift the flour with the salt. Add the sour cream or yogurt and knead lightly until a smooth, medium soft dough is formed. Cover and let rest for 30 minutes.

Some cooks say that you should use only cool water to make the softest dough. I have used slightly warm water, hot water, and cold water, but I have not noticed an appreciable difference; kneading the dough until it is smooth and elastic seems to matter a great deal—but do not knead beyond that, as it will toughen the dough.

4 cups flour

1 tsp salt

2 cups or more sour cream or plain yogurt

To Make the Perogies

Divide the dough into several pieces, each about three inches in diameter, or other manageable size. Knead and roll each piece into a flattened ball and dust well with flour before putting it into a bowl to rest, at least 30 minutes.

Roll out one dough ball at a time on a lightly floured board, using as little flour as possible to prevent the dough sticking to the board. The rolled dough should be about $\frac{1}{8}$ inch thick. Cover the uncut portion of dough with a cloth to prevent drying out. Cut the rolled out dough into squares of approximately $2\frac{1}{2}$ inches, or less, or into rounds if you prefer. Larger perogies are not as tasty as the ratio of filling to dough changes as the size changes.

Place a spoonful of filling (see Sauerkraut Fillings in index) on each piece, then fold the dough square into the traditional triangle or in a rectangle. Pinch the edges together to seal in the filling, making sure no filling has been caught between the edges. Place each completed triangle or rectangle on a clean towel, well spaced apart, so they do not stick to one another. If many are being made, cover the completed squares with another towel to keep the perogies from drying out. At this point, perogies may be frozen for future use. Lay the perogies in a single layer on a cookie sheet or tray, well spaced. Place in freezer for several hours, and when they are frozen, drop them into a plastic bag, sealing it tightly. Frozen perogies may be stored cooked or uncooked for 3-4 months.

Cooking the Perogies

Cook the perogies a few at a time in a pot of rapidly boiling, salted water. Stir with a wooden spoon, as a metal spoon will cut the dough. In a large pot, it is possible to cook between 30-50 at a time, but the perogies should not be overcrowded. The perogies will cook in about 8-10 minutes, and should be removed from the pot when they have puffed up and risen to the surface.

It is easier to remove the perogies from the pot if the boiling water is cooled somewhat with the addition of 1 cup cold water. Use a perforated spoon to transfer the perogies to a colander. Rinse with a little cold water and drain. Place a few cooked perogies in a small bowl. Sprinkle with salt and a spoonful or two of onion and bacon fried in butter. Toss to coat evenly, then put into a serving bowl, adding the remaining perogies as they are cooked. Keep in a warm oven, or warm them in the microwave for 3-4 minutes. Serve with sour cream.

Sometimes perogies are deep fat fried, in which case they do not need to be dressed with any butter, salad oil, or sour cream. If you wish to deep fry them, it is best to bring them to a boil first, then remove from the water. Allow to drain well, then finish them in a deep fat fryer, or in a skillet with an inch or so of cooking oil. Perogies may be dressed with any one of the following:

- a bit of salad oil and tossed gently to coat them well
- diced and fried salt pork
- chopped ham and onion fried together either in oil or butter, or a combination of the two
- Brown Buttered Crumbs; made with melted butter, heated until it begins to brown, adding fine, dried bread crumbs, and gently stir-frying until the crumbs are lightly toasted.

Cooking the Perogies

Problems

If the perogies fall apart during cooking, these may be the reasons for the problem:

- improper seal
- overcooking
- dough was too hard, dried out, or too soft to seal properly
- dough rolled too thinly

If perogies stick together:

- the water wasn't boiling
- they weren't stirred frequently enough
- too many perogies were in the pot

Leftover Perogies

Cooked perogies are even nicer the next day. If you have frozen them uncooked, drop them into boiling water to cook. Drain, and proceed as for freshly made perogies. Cooked frozen perogies do not need to be thawed out. Place them in a non-stick skillet and fry, covered, on low heat until they are hot and golden brown. Turn over and brown on the other side before serving. If you don't want them toasted, put them in the microwave for a couple of minutes.

Serve the perogies with sour cream. For a different flavor, add a spoonful of tart kalyna jelly or sauce, made of highbush cranberry, to the sour cream. Lingonberry jelly or sauce tastes just as good, but any tart jelly may be used.

Sauerkraut Filling

Cook the sauerkraut for about 15 minutes until softened. Drain the sauerkraut thoroughly, pressing out as much water as possible. In a large non-stick skillet, fry the onion and bacon, if using, until just turning golden.

Chop the sauerkraut finely, and add to the onion and bacon. Season to taste. Fry together about 10 minutes. Cool before using.

There are many other fillings for perogies. See the chapter on Fillings.

3 1/2 cups sauerkraut

2-3 Tbsp shortening or lard

1 medium onion, chopped

1/2 cup chopped bacon (optional)

salt and pepper to taste

Baking

Pancakes

Each European country has its version of the delicate, thin, filled pancakes. Some call them crepes, others rolled pancakes, while to Poles and Ukrainians they are nalysnyky, and to Russians, blini. By whatever name you call them, they are good to eat and worth making.

Recipes for these pancakes vary somewhat, but all agree that the batter should be very thin. The use of a little water in the batter is said to make the pancakes more tender. Fillings may be savory or sweet; they may be served with a variety of sauces, as a main course, or as a dessert.

Nalysnyky

12 (6-inch) pancakes

3 eggs

²/₃ cup all-purpose flour

¹/₂ tsp salt

1 cup milk

¹/₂ cup water

melted butter, cooking oil, or a mixture of both

The traditional filling for nalysnyky is cottage cheese, and they are eaten with sour cream, but any savory filling can be used to make a satisfying supper dish. This one uses a Sauerkraut-Mushroom filling.

Beat the eggs until light.

Add the remaining ingredients and beat the batter until smooth.

Using a small non-stick skillet, or a crepe pan 6-7 inches in diameter, preheat butter or oil lightly. Pour in 2 Tbsp of batter, tilt the pan back and forth to coat evenly. Cook over moderate heat until lightly browned on the bottom and firm on the top. Remove the pancake to a plate. Lightly butter the pan before adding the batter. While the second pancake is cooking, spread filling on the cooked pancake, roll it, and place in a prepared dish. If you wish to do all the pancakes before rolling them, put pieces of waxpaper between each pancake as it comes out of the pan.

Nalysnyky

Filling Technique

Regardless of the type of filling used, the technique for filling is the same: place the pancake brown side down on the plate, place a generous spoonful on the pancake, spreading it on the lower half of the pancake; roll it up, cut it in half and place it, seam side down, in a lightly buttered casserole, or baking dish, before filling the next one.

When all are filled, dot the pancakes with butter, and cook in a moderate oven, 350° F for 10-20 minutes, until well heated. Serve with appropriate sauces or sour cream.

Fluffy Nalysnyky

12 (6-inch) pancakes

To make a fluffier batter, use the same ingredients as the previous recipe, but separate the eggs, beating the egg whites until stiff. Set aside.

Following the previous recipe, beat the egg yolks, adding the remaining ingredients. Fold in the beaten egg whites last.

Layered Nalysnyky

4 cups well-drained sauerkraut

3 Tbsp shortening or bacon fat

1 medium onion, minced

1 cup finely chopped mushrooms

3 Tbsp sour cream

1 Tbsp dill (optional)

caraway seeds to taste (optional)

Leave each pancake flat. Spread with filling (recipe follows), then top with another pancake, alternating the filling and the pancakes. When the stack is the desired depth, butter the top pancake and place in a moderate oven, 350° F, to heat through, about 20-25 minutes. Cut into wedges to serve.

Sauerkraut And Mushroom Filling

Chop the sauerkraut very finely. In a large skillet, melt the shortening, fry the bacon and onions until translucent. Add the mushrooms, cooking until they begin to wilt. Add the sauerkraut, sour cream, salt and pepper, and dill, or caraway seed if you prefer. Stir together and fry until the sauerkraut is softened and the flavors are blended. Chill the filling before using.

15-20 pancakes

Potato-Sauerkraut Pancakes

2 cups drained sauerkraut

1-2 cups water

5 cups grated raw potatoes (8-9 medium potatoes), kept in water so as not to discolor

2 medium onions, minced

2 cups all-purpose flour

$1/2$ tsp salt

$1/2$ tsp pepper

$1/4$ cup milk

Potato pancakes are great favorites of mine. Combined with sauerkraut, they are even more special for supper or as a snack, with sour cream, apple sauce, or melted butter and fried bacon and onions.

Put the sauerkraut in a pot with the water and bring to a boil. Simmer for a few minutes, until it is limp. Drain the sauerkraut and squeeze it dry. Grind or chop it very finely. Set aside.

Drain potatoes and put them into a large bowl with the sauerkraut and minced onions, the flour, the salt and pepper, and milk. Stir to mix well. Add a bit more milk if necessary to make a batter about the thickness of sour cream.

Drop by tablespoonful onto a hot, oiled griddle and spread flat. Brown on both sides. Serve hot.

Breads, Buns, and Cakes

Although sauerkraut may seem an unlikely baking addition, it makes an interesting contribution to a variety of buns, breads, strudels, and even cakes. It is usually used as a filling, but in one case, at least, it is the secret ingredient in a truly magnificent cake.

In some of the following recipes, any of the fillings—sour or sweet—I have included in the Fillings section of *Discovering Sauerkraut* may be used; in others, I have recommended certain fillings.

Basic Sweet Yeast Dough

Dissolve the yeast in a $^1/_2$ cup of warm water together with the ginger. Pour the scalded milk into a warmed bowl; add the salt, sugar, and butter, stirring until they are incorporated into the milk. Cool to lukewarm.

In a large mixing bowl, combine the yeast, the milk mixture, and 2 cups of flour. Beat until well mixed. Set aside in a warm place until it is light and bubbly.

Beat the eggs and egg yolks, and stir into the batter. Beat 2-3 cups of flour, or more, into the batter to form a smooth, light dough. Turn the dough onto a floured board, and knead it until smooth and elastic, and it forms blisters. Shape into a ball and place in a clean, floured bowl. Cover with a towel and put into a warm, draft-free place to rise until doubled in bulk, about 1 to 1 $^1/_2$ hours.

Punch dough down and knead lightly. Let the dougl rest for about 30 minutes; then roll into a rectangle to fit a cookie sheet. Let rise again for 30 minutes.

Preheat oven to 400° F.

Spread the cooled chosen filling on top of the raised dough (see Fillings for choices). Let it rise again for 20-30 minutes. Place in the oven and bake for about 20 minutes, or until the dough is crisp and brown, and the filling is baked into it.

2 pkgs fresh or powdered yeast

$^1/_2$ cup warm water

$^1/_2$ tsp powdered ginger

1 cup milk, scalded

1 tsp salt

$^1/_2$ cup sugar

$^1/_2$ cup soft butter

4-5 cups all-purpose flour

2 whole eggs

4 egg yolks

Sauerkraut Coffee Cake

1 recipe Basic Yeast Dough, without sugar or lemon

6 cups rinsed sauerkraut, squeezed dry

$^1/_2$ cup butter or bacon fat, softened

$^1/_2$ cup diced bacon

1 onion, diced

salt and pepper to taste

1 Tbsp chopped dill

1 tsp caraway seeds (optional)

1 cup chopped ham

2 Tbsp all-purpose flour

milk to mix

3-4 Tbsp sour cream

The dough in this recipe may be used for other sweet pastries. If you want to use nuts, raisins, dried fruit, grated lemon or orange, add these ingredients to the dough when you punch it down after the first rising. Let the dough rest about 30 minutes; then shape as desired, and continue with the directons here.

Prepare the dough, using only 3 cups of flour. When it has risen once, punch it down; then roll it out to fit a cookie sheet. Let it rise again for 20-30 minutes.

Preheat oven to 400° F.

Chop the sauerkraut finely. In a large skillet, heat the butter or bacon fat and fry the diced bacon and onion until they begin to turn golden. Add the sauerkraut, with salt and pepper to taste, dill, and caraway seeds. Mix well, then stir in the ham. Cover, cooking slowly and stirring occasionally to prevent burning.

Make a smooth paste of 2 Tbsp flour and a little milk, and stir into the hot sauerkraut. Simmer for a few minutes to cook the flour and thicken the sauerkraut mixture. Add the sour cream. Correct the seasoning. Let cool to warm before using the filling.

Basic Dough for Filled Buns

about 70 (2-inch) buns

This Ukrainian version of Basic Bun Dough is very rich and is used with savory or sweet fillings. This dough needs a lot of kneading to develop the richness and fine texture. I use a Cabbage and Ham filling.

Scald the milk; add the $^1/_2$ cup butter, and cool to lukewarm.

In a small bowl, put in the $^1/_2$ tsp sugar and $^1/_2$ tsp ginger along with the lukewarm water. Sprinkle the yeast on top.

When the yeast is softened, put into a large bowl and add $^1/_2$ cup of the milk-butter mixture. Add 1 cup flour and beat until smooth. Let the batter stand in a warm place until it begins to bubble.

Add the sugar-egg yolks mixture to the batter, together with the rest of the milk and vanilla. Add 1 $^1/_2$ cups of flour to the batter and beat until smooth. Add 3 egg whites beaten stiff, mix; then add enough flour to make a soft dough. Knead for 15 minutes; then add $^1/_4$ cup of melted butter, and knead until all trace of butter disappears. Continue adding flour and kneading until you have a smooth, elastic dough; then knead for 10-25 minutes more. Let rise in a warm place until doubled in bulk, about 1 to 1 $^1/_2$ hours.

Divide dough into 6 portions. Make each portion into a roll 1 $^1/_4$ inches in diameter. Cut each roll into 1-inch pieces.

Preheat oven to 350° F.

Flatten each piece and brush with the remaining 2 stiffly beaten egg whites. Top each piece of dough with 1 tsp filling (recipe follows), and pinch the edges together to form a ball. Place the balls, with the pinched side down, into a well-greased pan and let rise in a warm place until it is doubled in bulk.

Brush buns with the remaining beaten egg whites. Put the buns into the oven and lower the heat to 300° F. Bake for 15-20 minutes until golden brown. If you would like a nice topping, mix some crushed walnuts with sugar and sprinkle over the top of the buns after brushing with the egg.

1 $^1/_2$ cups scalded milk cooled to lukewarm

$^1/_2$ cup butter, melted

$^1/_2$ cup lukewarm water

$^1/_2$ tsp sugar

$^1/_2$ tsp ginger

2 Tbsp or 2 pkgs dry active yeast

5 $^1/_2$ to 6 cups all-purpose or unbleached flour

$^1/_4$ to $^1/_2$ cup sugar beaten with 5 egg yolks

1 tsp vanilla

1 tsp salt

5 egg whites

$^1/_4$ cup melted butter

(continued)

Basic Dough for Filled Buns

4 Tbsp butter or bacon fat

1 onion, diced

1 medium head cabbage, shredded and chopped fine, or 3 cups sauerkraut, squeezed dry, or half cabbage, half sauerkraut (optional)

1 cup ground or finely chopped cooked ham

1 tsp lemon juice

1 Tbsp chopped dill

salt and pepper to taste

2-3 Tbsp sour cream

Cabbage And Ham Filling

In a large non-stick skillet, fry the onion gently in butter or bacon fat until it is softened. Add the cabbage or sauerkraut and fry until it is limp. Add the ham, lemon juice, dill, salt and pepper. Stir and fry gently until the cabbage is cooked. Add sour cream if using. Chill before using.

Buns, Pyrih, and Pyrizhky

(6 portions)

Slavs like to make small filled pastries or buns known as pyrizhky or pyrih which are often used as hors d'oeuvres. Both are made with the same dough. Pyrizhky are bun-like while a pyrih is made more in the style of a pie or roll which is served cut up.

Fillings vary considerably from savory to sweet. All are tasty. This dough recipe will make 3 bread loaves; a pyrih with a cabbage, sauerkraut, or cheese filling; a pan of filled buns; and some pyrizhky with a filling. You can also use this dough to make Surprise Buns (see index), or you can use your own favorite bread dough recipe.

Dissolve $1/2$ tsp sugar and mix with the ginger in $1/2$ cup of warm water. Sprinkle the yeast on top and let stand until the yeast is light and bubbly.

In a large warm bowl, combine the scalded milk and 4 cups warm water. Add the melted butter, yeast mixture, and 6 cups of flour. Beat to make a smooth batter. Let the batter stand in a warm place until it is light and has risen to double its original bulk, about 1 hour.

Add the salt, beaten eggs, sugar, and the remaining flour to the batter. Knead well until smooth and elastic, and the dough falls away from the hands.

Place the dough in a greased bowl and brush the top with oil or melted butter. Cover and return to a warm place to rise until double in bulk, about 2 hours.

Punch the dough down. Place on a floured board and divide into 6 equal portions.

$1/2$ cup warm water

$1/2$ tsp sugar

$1/2$ tsp ginger

2 Tbsp or 2 pkgs active dry yeast

2 cups scalded milk

$1/4$ cup melted butter

4 cups warm water

6 cups all-purpose or unbleached flour

2 Tbsp salt

4 eggs, beaten

7-8 cups flour

2-3 Tbsp oil or melted butter

Buns, Pyrih, and Pyrizhky

Loaves

The loaves are not filled, but go nicely with many of the dishes in this book.

Make 3 portions into mounds. Let rest about 10 minutes. Flatten or roll a mound into a rectangle wider and longer than the pan you will bake it in. Roll the rectangle tightly and tuck in the sides to fit the well-greased pan, making sure it touches the ends of the pan. Brush the top with oil or butter; cover with a slightly dampened cloth, and place in a warm place to rise until doubled in bulk.

Preheat oven to 400° F.

Bake the loaves for 10 minutes then reduce heat to 350° F and bake for another 30-40 minutes until the loaves are browned and shrunk away from the sides of the pan.

To test for doneness, turn out one loaf from the pan and tap the underside. If it sounds hollow, the bread is ready. If it is not quite well baked, return it to the oven for a few minutes longer.

To Make a Braided loaf:

Divide one mound of dough into 3 balls. Roll each ball into a cylinder 12 inches long; braid the 3 lengths together and tuck both ends under. Proceed as for other loaves.

Pyrih

Take half of the dough and roll it into a square about $^1/_2$ inch thick. Dimensions will vary with the amount of dough you have. In the centre, place half the recipe for a sauerkraut filling (see index), or one of your own choice. Bring the corners in the centre and seal the edges. Turn the pyrih onto a well-greased pie plate or baking pan, with the sealed edges down. Prick the pastry with a fork to let any steam escape. Repeat with the rest of the dough.

Put the pyrih in a warm place to rise until double in bulk. Brush with beaten egg and bake for 30-45 minutes. Serve as is, or with sour cream.

Buns, Pyrih, and Pyrizhky (continued)

Pyrizhky

Roll half of dough into a rectangle (size will vary with the amount of dough you have) about $1/2$ inch thick, and cut into squares of 2 $1/2$ to 3 inches. Place a spoonful of Sauerkraut Mushroom Filling (see index), or the one you prefer, on each square and fold over to make a triangle. Seal the edges by pinching them firmly together. Place the triangles on a greased pan and let rise until doubled in bulk. Repeat with the rest of the dough or use it for another recipe.

Brush with beaten egg and bake for 25 minutes. Serve with sour cream, if desired.

Raised Sauerkraut Roll

Put the yeast into a small bowl with $1/2$ cup warm water to which have been added the $1/2$ tsp sugar and the ginger. Stir to dissolve and let stand for 10- 15 minutes until the yeast begins to bubble.

Sift the flour into a large bowl; make a hollow in the centre, and pour in the remaining water with the yeast mixture. Mix all together and let rest about 20 minutes in a warm place. Beat together the eggs, salt, sugar, and melted butter. Pour over the dough, and keep kneading until it is smooth and elastic and the dough comes off your hands. Let rise for 45-60 minutes until doubled in bulk.

Preheat oven to 350° F.

Roll dough flat and spread with Sauerkraut Filling No. 5 (see index), or one you prefer. Roll up jelly-roll fashion and let rest for 20-30 minutes.

Bake for 45 minutes until browned or sounds hollow when tapped on the bottom.

2 Tbsp or 2 pkgs active dry yeast

1 $3/4$ cups warm water

$1/2$ tsp sugar

$1/2$ tsp powdered ginger

3 Tbsp melted butter

3 cups all-purpose or unbleached flour

3 eggs

$1/2$ tsp salt

2-3 Tbsp sugar

Surprise Buns

1 recipe raised bread or bun dough

1/2 cup diced bacon

1 cup chopped onion

1 cup peeled, chopped tomatoes

2 1/2 to 3 cups drained sauerkraut, finely chopped

1 Tbsp chopped dill

salt and pepper to taste

2 cups chopped, cooked chicken or ham

When my mother baked bread, she sometimes also made sweet buns. If she didn't have time to make a batch of sweet dough, she would make a pan of buns out of regular dough. She made a filling of sauerkraut and often added leftover meat to make them different.

Fry the bacon slowly in a large skillet with the butter until it becomes translucent. Add the onion, tomatoes, sauerkraut, the mushrooms, and dill, and season with salt and pepper to taste. Fry slowly until the mixture begins to change color and the sauerkraut is tender. Add the chicken or ham, and stir to mix well. Cool before using.

Preheat oven to 350° F.

Cut the raised dough into pieces the size of a large orange. Roll each piece into an oval shape. Put some of the filling in the centre of the dough. Bring in the long edges together and close the seam. Place in a well-greased pan, seam side down, well spaced. Let rise for 30-45 minutes.

Bake for 20-30 minutes.

Pagachi

Russians and the inhabitants of the former Yugoslavia and Macedonia make pies of yeast-raised dough filled with a wide choice of fillings, including sauerkraut. The pies—pagachi in Russia or if they are bun-shaped are called hadzimka, and zelnik in Macedonia—are served as snacks or for light meals. There are several recipes for the dough, each slightly different from the others. Where the recipe makes a large amount, as in the following pagachi, the recipe may be halved.

Dissolve the yeast in the warm water, with $^1/_2$ tsp sugar, and ginger. Stir together the lukewarm water or milk, sugar, salt, oil, 3 $^1/_2$ cups flour, and the proofed yeast mixture. Mix well. Add the rest of the flour to make a soft dough. Turn out onto a floured board and knead for about 10 minutes. Place dough in a greased bowl. Cover and let rise until doubled in bulk.

Preheat oven to 400° F.

Take a portion of dough, a ball about 3 inches in diameter, and flatten it with your hand. Place about a cupful of Sauerkraut Filling No. 4 (see index), or whichever one you prefer, in the middle of the dough circle. Seal. Turn ball over, seam side down, and press carefully with the hands to flatten down to about $^3/_8$ inch thick. Flatten gently, taking care that the filling is not squeezed out. Place on a cookie sheet and prick in a few places with a fork.

Place the cookie sheet on the lowest shelf in the oven and bake for approximately 10 minutes. Remove from oven and turn the pagachi over. Return to the oven and bake for another 5 minutes. The dough should be a light brown. Remove from the oven and brush the top with melted butter.

2 Tbsp or 2 pkgs active, dry yeast

$^1/_2$ cup warm water

$^1/_2$ tsp sugar

$^1/_2$ tsp ginger

1 $^3/_4$ cups lukewarm water or milk

3 Tbsp sugar

1 Tbsp salt

4 Tbsp salad oil

7 cups all-purpose or unbleached flour

melted butter

Hadzimka

¹/₂ tsp sugar

1 tsp salt

¹/₂ cup lukewarm water

1 Tbsp or 1 pkg active dry or fresh yeast

1 ¹/₂ cups scalded milk,

¹/₂ cup margarine, melted

5 cups all-purpose or unbleached sifted flour

1 recipe Sauerkraut filling (see index)

2 Tbsp sugar

In a large bowl,!add ¹/₂ tsp sugar and salt to the water. Sprinkle in the yeast and let stand until bubbly. Add the lukewarm milk, 2 Tbsp sugar, margarine, and stir. Add sifted flour, using your hands to mix until a soft dough is formed and it leaves the sides of the bowl and your hands. Cover with a cloth and put in a warm place to rise until doubled in bulk, about 1 hour. Punch down the dough and return, covered, to a warm place to rise again, about 1 hour.

Preheat oven to 375° F.

Place on a floured board and divide into 6 parts, rounding each piece into a ball. Flatten each ball, put filling in centre, fold over and seal. Flatten each filled ball as much as possible, without squeezing out the filling.

Place on a large, well-greased cookie sheet and bake hadzimka until light brown on both sides.

Serve warm and buttered.

Zelnik

Zelnik may sound just like Russian pagachi, but the dough is prepared more like that for French croissants, giving it a much different texture. A traditional sauerkraut filling is given below, but you can create a filling of spinach, meats, green peppers and onions, cottage cheese, potatoes and cheddar cheese, or use your favorite sauerkraut filling.

Using a warm bowl, dissolve the yeast in the cup of warm water with $1/2$ tsp sugar added. Add the salt and oil and stir until well mixed. Add 2 cups flour and beat until smooth. Add the beaten eggs and blend well. Blend in 2 more cups of flour, adding more if needed to make a soft dough that leaves the sides of the bowl. Turn out onto a floured board and knead until smooth and elastic, about 10 minutes. Divide the dough into two smooth balls. Place on the floured board and cover with a large bowl or slightly dampened towel. Let stand for 10-15 minutes.

Preheat oven to 300° F.

Roll out one ball of dough to a rectangle 11 inches by 14 inches. Brush with melted butter, fold in half, roll out again; repeat the buttering and rolling 4-5 times. Then roll out again to a rectangle 16 inches by 11 inches. Place on a well-greased pan 15 $1/2$ inches by 10 $1/2$ inches. The dough should overlap the edges of the pan. Spread the filling. Roll out the second ball of dough as directed above. Place on top of the filling. Roll edges to seal and brush top with butter.

Bake for 45 minutes or until golden brown.

1 Tbsp or 1 pkg compressed or active dry yeast

1 cup warm water

$1/2$ tsp sugar

1 $1/2$ tsp salt

2 Tbsp oil

4 to 4 $1/2$ cups all-purpose or unbleached flour, sifted

2 eggs, well beaten

$1/4$ cup butter or margarine, melted

Sauerkraut Filling (recipe follows)

(continued)

Zelnik

2 Tbsp butter or margarine

2 1/2 cups rinsed, drained sauerkraut, chopped fine

1/2 tsp paprika

1 tsp chopped dill

2 eggs, well beaten

Sauerkraut Filling

In large skillet, melt the butter and add the sauerkraut. Fry until the sauerkraut is limp and starting to change color. Add the paprika and dill. Stir well and cool. Add the well-beaten eggs and mix well.

Variation: Make individual pastries by rolling the dough only 3/4 inch thick. Cut into 4-inch squares, put a spoonful of filling inside, fold over and seal. Let rise until doubled in bulk. Preheat oven to 350° F. Brush the raised pastries with melted butter and bake for 30 minutes until golden brown.

Sauerkraut Pirogen

1 egg, beaten

1/2 cup plain yogurt

2 Tbsp melted margarine

1/2 tsp salt

1 1/2 cups all-purpose or unbleached sifted flour

milk or diluted egg for top

If you lack time to make yeast-raised dough, here is a dough of Jewish origin which can be made in a hurry. Pirogen are like turnovers. If you wish, substitute a Butter Pastry or your favorite short crust. Sauerkraut with Dried Fruit Filling (see index) is good in pirogen.

Preheat oven to 375° F.

Mix the egg, the yogurt, margarine, salt, and flour, combining well. Chill for 20-30 minutes in the refrigerator. Roll the dough thinly, and cut into 6-inch rounds, smaller if desired. Put a spoonful or more filling on each round. Fold over to make a half moon and seal the edges with a fork. Brush the tops with milk or beaten egg diluted with a spoonful of water.

Bake on a greased cookie sheet for about 30 minutes.

Half Moon Pyrizhky

36 buns

Pyrizhky, or filled buns, are very popular and there are numerous ways of making them. Here is a slightly different and smaller recipe than most.

Dissolve $^1/_2$ tsp sugar in $^1/_2$ cup warm water, add the ginger; sprinkle on the yeast and let stand 10-15 minutes for the yeast to start bubbling.

To the scalded milk, add the other $^1/_2$ cup warm water, butter, salt, eggs, and 2 tsp sugar; add the yeast mixture, then about half of the flour. Beat thoroughly to make a batter. Gradually add the remaining flour and knead well. Cover, and let stand in a warm place to rise until the dough doubles in bulk, about 1 to 1 $^1/_2$ hours.

Preheat oven to 350° F.

Make the dough into a roll 1 inch in diameter; cut roll into 1 $^1/_2$ inch pieces; form each piece into a ball; flatten each ball and put 1 tsp of filling (Sauerkraut and Apple Filling, see index) in the centre. Fold once over the filling. Seal by pinching the edges together. Place sealed side down in a well-greased pan. Let rise until doubled in bulk.

Brush the pyrizhky with the beaten egg and water. Bake for 25 minutes. Serve with sour cream or a warm Smetana Sauce (see index).

$^1/_2$ cup warm water

$^1/_2$ tsp sugar

$^1/_2$ tsp ginger

1 pkg quick rising yeast

1 cup scalded milk

$^1/_2$ cup warm water

$^1/_2$ cup melted butter

1 $^1/_2$ tsp salt

4 eggs, beaten

2 tsp sugar

5 to 6 $^1/_2$ cups all-purpose or unbleached flour

1 egg beaten with 1 tsp water

Sauerkraut Strudel

Homemade Noodle Dough

¹/₄ lb chopped or ground ham, cooked chicken, or fried bacon

Sauerkraut and Apple Filling (see index), cooked until no liquid remains

water or stock

paprika

2-3 Tbsp sour cream

Savory or sweet strudels are enjoyed in many countries, as any good pastry should be. This one is made with Homemade Noodle Dough (see index), but try different recipes until you find one you like.

After the well-kneaded dough has rested, divide it into 3-4 portions. Roll into very thin sheets. Let the dough dry for 10-15 minutes, but do not let it get brittle. Preheat the oven to 375° F.

Place a semi-dried dough sheet on a board. Sprinkle with chopped or ground meat, then some of the sauerkraut filling. Roll the sheet carefully, jelly-roll style. Cut across diagonally about 2 ¹/₂ inches apart to make individual pieces. Flatten slightly with your hand, and place in a well-buttered pan, side by side without crowding. Cover with foil wrap if the pan has no lid. Brown on the stove top gently, turning once. When both sides are brown, add a little water or stock, just enough to cover the bottom of the pan.

Bake until the dough is baked through. Remove the strudel pieces from the pan and keep warm. Serve with a sauce made from pan juices with added paprika for coloring, and 2-3 Tbsp sour cream. Heat but do not let it boil. Spoon over the strudel. Alternatively, serve with Dill Sauce, (see index).

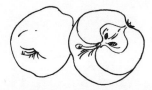

Yeast Strudel Dough

There are many kinds of dough for strudels, some yeast raised, some needing to be stretched.

Preheat oven to 350° F.

Cut the flour, 1 cup of butter or margarine, and salt together, as for pastry. Have the sour cream and egg yolks at room temperature. Dissolve the yeast in the sour cream and add to the flour-butter mixture, along with the egg yolks. Combine thoroughly, and knead until the mixture is smooth. Place dough in a bowl, brush with remaining butter or margarine, and chill for 8 hours or overnight. When ready to use, place dough on a lightly floured boerd, and pat it down. Then turn it over so both sides are floured. Using a rolling pin, roll the dough as thinly as possible. It will make a long, very thin sheet of dough which may be halved to make two strudels. Spread the dough with filling, keeping filling at least 1 inch in from the edges. Fold the sides over the filling; then roll the dough carefully, jelly roll fashion, and seal the edges so that the filling doesn't seep out. Lift the roll carefully onto a shallow baking pan.

Bake the strudel for 50-60 minutes, or until browned and well cooked.

2¹/₂ cups all-purpose or unbleached flour

5 ¹/₄ cups butter or margarine

¹/₂ tsp salt

¹/₂ cup sour cream

3 large egg yolks

1 Tbsp or envelope of active dry yeast

Sauerkraut and Apricot Filling (see index)

Stretched Strudel Dough

2 ½ cups all-purpose flour

1 tsp salt

3 Tbsp margarine or cooking oil (not olive oil)

2 eggs, beaten

⅔ cup lukewarm water

melted butter

This method of making strudel dough is time-consuming, but it makes the finest of all strudels. This delicate pastry melts in one's mouth!

In a large bowl, mix the flour, salt, margarine or oil, eggs, and water. Knead very well; then beat with a rolling pin, or lift up and lash against the table edge. Allow the dough to rest in a warm place for about 15 minutes.

Cover a table, (preferably a round one) with a clean cloth, and dust it with flour. Roll out the dough and put it in the middle of the table, then stretch it on the backs of your hands until it is paper thin. Do not try to patch up holes if they appear. Brush the stretched dough with melted butter if it is drying too fast. Cut away thick edges.

Preheat oven to 450° F.

Place the filling along one edge of the dough; sprinkle with melted butter, and use the cloth to roll up the strudel. Fold in the edges. The last roll of the cloth should place the strudel on a well-buttered baking sheet. Bake the strudel for 10 minutes; reduce the heat to 400° F and bake for another 20 minutes. Reduce heat again to 350° F and bake until completely cooked, about 20 minutes.

Deep-Fried Buns

about 140 (2-inch) buns

Doughnuts and other fried goodiew are enjoyed by all. Best of all, however, are these deep-fried filled buns. Try them with your favorite sauerkraut filling, or experiment with a sweet filling. Each bite calls for more!

Mix the water, 1/2 tsp sugar, and ginger in a small bowl. Sprinkle with yeast, and let the mixture stand until the yeast begins to bubble, about 10-15 minutes.

Put 10 cups of flour in a large bowl; add the 2 tsp sugar and the salt; mix. Add the cooled milk and the melted butter to the beaten eggs. Make a well in the flour, and add the milk and egg mixture all at once. Mix in the proofed yeast. Stir until a soft dough is formed, adding a little flour as needed. When the dough leaves the sides of the bowl, turn it onto a floured board, and knead until it is smooth and elastic. Dust the bowl with flour; return the dough to the bowl. Cover with a towel, and set in a warm place until doubled in bulk. Punch down and let rise again.

Cut off small egg-size pieces of dough; flatten or roll out each one, to about 2 1/2 to 3 inches in diameter; add a teaspoonful of filling, and seal the edges. Place the sealed sides down on a floured board or on towels, and let rise for 1 hour until the buns are doubled in bulk.

Deep fry in hot oil, 375° F on frying thermometer until the buns are golden brown on both sides. If you have no deep fryer or thermometer, you can test the temperature of the fat by dropping in a piece of bread. If it browns in 60 seconds, the fat is hot enough.

1 cup lukewarm water

1/2 tsp sugar

1/2 tsp ginger

3 Tbsp or envelopes of active dry yeast

10 to 11 cups all-purpose or unbleached flour

2 tsp sugar

oil or fat for frying

2 tsp salt

6 eggs, beaten

2 cups scalded milk, cooled to lukewarm

3/4 cup melted butter or margarine

your favorite sauerkraut filling (see index)

Sauerkraut Pie

3 cups sauerkraut

2-3 cups soup stock,
consommé, or water

$^1/_2$ cup diced bacon

1 onion, diced

1 Tbsp butter or oil

pie pastry

4-5 Bavarian smokies, or
spicy, smoked sausages

2 eggs

1 cup light cream

4 Tbsp chili sauce

2 tsp paprika

salt and pepper to taste

This savory dish is not quite a pie, not quite a quiche, but it makes a very acceptable lunch or supper.

Add the sauerkraut to the soup stock, bring to a boil, reduce heat, and simmer for 20-30 minutes until the sauerkraut is cooked. Drain the sauerkraut, and squeeze it dry. Set aside. In a small skillet, fry the bacon and onion in butter or oil until they begin to change color.

Preheat oven to 350° F.

Line a deep pie plate with pastry. Add a layer of sauerkraut, then a layer of bacon and onion. Split the smokies lengthwise and place on the bacon and onion layers.

Beat the eggs with the light cream, the chili sauce, the paprika, and the seasonings. Pour over the layers in the pie plate. Bake for 35-45 minutes until the custard has set. To test the custard for doneness, insert a knife tip in the centre of the pie. The pie is cooked if no trace of custard remains on the knife when it is withdrawn.

Sauerkraut Surprise Cake

This chocolate cake may be the biggest surprise of all. It may have been invented by German immigrants to North America, but whoever made it first had a great idea. The sauerkraut imparts no discernible flavor but provides a coconut-like texture.

Have all ingredients at room temperature.
Preheat oven to 350° F.

Sift all the dry ingredients into a bowl. In another bowl, cream the margarine until fluffy, adding the sugar gradually. Cream until light. Add the eggs, one at a time, and beat well between additions. Add the vanilla and blend. Stir in the flour mixture alternately with the orange juice, beginning and ending with the flour mixture.

Snip the sauerkraut into smaller pieces with a pair of scissors or chop fine with a meat cleaver. Add the sauerkraut and walnuts to the batter. Turn the batter into two buttered and floured 8-inch round tins, tapping bottoms lightly to release excess air. Bake for 30-35 minutes or until the cakes test done. Cool in pan for 5 minutes before turning out to cool on wire racks.

Frost with Sour Cream Chocolate Frosting (recipe follows).

2 cups plus 2 Tbsp sifted all-purpose or unbleached flour

1 tsp baking soda

1 tsp baking powder

1/2 cup Dutch cocoa

1/4 tsp salt

1/2 cup margarine or butter

2 cups brown sugar

3 large eggs

1 tsp vanilla

1 cup orange juice

2/3 cup, rinsed, well drained sauerkraut

3/4 cup chopped walnuts

Sour Cream Chocolate Frosting

Enough to fill and frost two 9-inch rounds or a 10-inch tube cake.

Combine chocolate chips and butter or margarine in the top of the double boiler, and melt over hot but not boiling water. Remove from heat and cool slightly. Blend in the sour cream, vanilla, and *1/4* tsp salt.

Gradually beat in enough of the icing sugar to make an easily-spread frosting.

9 oz semi-sweet chocolate chips

1/3 cup butter or margarine

3/4 cup sour cream

1 tsp vanilla

1/4 tsp salt

3 1/2 to 4 1/2 cups sifted icing sugar

Carob Sauerkraut Cake

2 $^{1}/_{8}$ cups unbleached sifted flour

$^{1}/_{2}$ cup carob powder

$^{1}/_{4}$ tsp salt

1 tsp baking powder

1 tsp baking soda

1 tsp cinnamon

$^{2}/_{3}$ scant cup margarine or butter

1 cup sugar

1 tsp vanilla

4 medium-size eggs

1 cup apple juice

$^{3}/_{4}$ cup carob chips

$^{2}/_{3}$ cups rinsed, drained, sauerkraut, chopped

An excellent cake for the health conscious! A delightful change from the usual chocolate cake, it makes use of sauerkraut and apple juice as well as carob chips and cinnamon.

Sift the first 6 ingredients in a medium-sized bowl. Sift together. In another bowl, cream margarine or butter, sugar, vanilla, and add the eggs, one at a time, beating well between additions. Add the dry ingredients alternately with the apple juice to the creamed mixture, ending with the dry mixture. Add the carob chips and sauerkraut to the mixture.

Preheat oven to 350° F.

Butter and flour a 9-inch by 13-inch cake pan and pour in the batter. Spread to reach the sides. Tap lightly on the bottom to release excess air. Bake for 30 minutes, or until cake tests done.

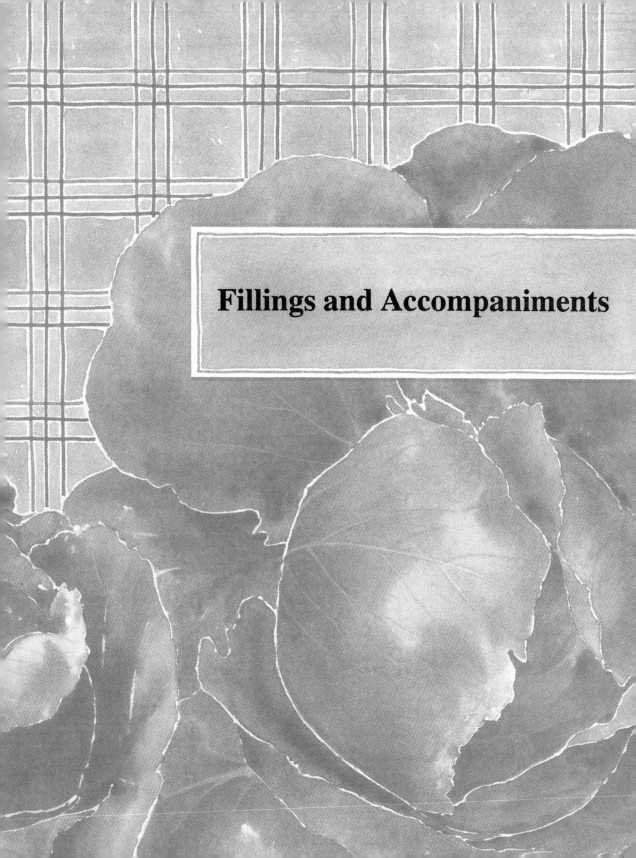

Fillings and Accompaniments

Fillings and Accompaniments

S avory fillings may be used in a wide variety of cooked and baked goods, such as *pyrohy*—or perogies as they are known in North America—*pyrizhky, vareniky, pagachi, zelnik,* filled buns, or anywhere you may need an unsweetened filling.

Sauerkraut fillings are made in many different ways and can be varied in any way you like. The most important thing is that they taste good. Some fillings are simple, such as Sauerkraut Filling No. 1. Long ago, many cooks used lard in cooking, as it made cooled sauerkraut fillings easier to use. I prefer oil.

While most of the recipes call for rinsed and well-drained sauerkraut, as well as added salt, your discretion must be used. Rinsed sauerkraut loses flavor, so rinse it only when it is strong flavored. Usually the sauerkraut is drained unless you need the extra liquid in the cooking. Even if the recipe calls for salt, the sauerkraut or prepared dish should be tasted before adding salt as sometimes the sauerkraut is salty enough.

Sauerkraut Filling No. 1

2 cups rinsed, drained sauerkraut

1 generous tsp butter, oil, margarine, bacon fat, or lard

In a medium-sized skillet, fry the sauerkraut in butter or other fat for 10-15 minutes, until it becomes limp. Cool before using.

Sauerkraut Filling No. 2

Chop the sauerkraut finely. In a large skillet or saucepan, cook onion in the fat until tender. Add the sauerkraut and sour cream, and season to taste. Cook over low heat, stirring occasionally, for 15-20 minutes, or until the sauerkraut is tender, and the flavors are blended. Do not overcook. Chill thoroughly before using.

2 to 2 1/2 cups rinsed, drained sauerkraut

1 medium onion, minced

4 Tbsp bacon fat or butter

3 Tbsp sour cream

salt and pepper to taste

Sauerkraut Filling No. 3

In a skillet, fry the bacon until the fat is released. Add the onion, and fry until it is soft. Add the 2 Tbsp cooking oil if needed. Add the sauerkraut and caraway seeds; stir to mix and cook a few minutes longer. Remove from heat, spoon sour cream into it, and stir thoroughly. Cool before using.

3 strips bacon, diced

1 medium onion, minced

2 Tbsp cooking oil

3 cups drained sauerkraut

1/2 tsp caraway seeds

1/4 cup sour cream

Sauerkraut Filling No. 4

1 onion, chopped

3 Tbsp butter

2 cups rinsed, drained sauerkraut

1 apple, chopped

dash of pepper

1 Tbsp brown sugar

salt to taste

In a large skillet, fry the onion in the butter, and when it begins to change color, add the sauerkraut and apple. Cook over low heat for about 20 minutes. Add the pepper, brown sugar, salt if needed, and continue cooking until the sauerkraut is golden. Cool before using.

Sauerkraut Filling No. 5

4 slices bacon, diced

1 cup chopped onon

3 cups rinsed sauerkraut, squeezed dry

2 apples, diced

$^1/_2$ cup chopped celery

1 Tbsp chopped parsley

In a large skillet, fry the bacon and onion until their color begins to change. Add the sauerkraut to the pan together with the remaining ingredients. Simmer until the sauerkraut is just cooked and starting to change color. Cool before using.

Sauerkraut Filling No. 6

Melt the butter in a large non-stick skillet. Add all the ingredients, and fry slowly over low heat until the sauerkraut is cooked, stirring often to prevent burning. Cool before using.

2 Tbsp butter or margarine

2 apples, chopped

6 green onions with tops, chopped

¹/₂ cup chopped ham

3 cups drained sauerkraut

2 Tbsp brown sugar

Sauerkraut Filling No. 7

Place the sauerkraut in a saucepan, add half the oil, the tomato paste, and dilute the mixture with stock or water. Simmer, adding the carrots, parsnip, onions, salt, sugar, and peppercorns. Continue cooking until all the liquid is absorbed, and the vegetables are cooked. Cool.

4 cups sauerkraut, squeezed dry

2 Tbsp cooking oil

1 ¹/₂ Tbsp tomato paste

1 ¹/₂ Tbsp stock or water

3 Tbsp grated carrot

3 Tbsp grated parsnip

2 onions, chopped

salt to taste

1 Tbsp sugar

4 peppercorns

Sauerkraut Filling No. 8

3 cups rinsed, drained
sauerkraut

2 Tbsp butter or margarine

¹/₂ tsp paprika

1 tsp chopped dill

salt and pepper to taste

2 eggs, well beaten

Put the sauerkraut into a non-stick skillet with the butter; sprinkle with paprika and chopped dill, adding salt if necessary and pepper to taste. On low heat, fry the sauerkraut slowly until it is limp. Cool, then add the beaten eggs to the sauerkraut. Mix thoroughly.

Sauerkraut Filling No. 9

3 Tbsp butter

3 cups rinsed, drained
sauerkraut

1 onion, minced

¹/₂ tsp sugar

salt to taste

¹/₂ tsp pepper or to taste

¹/₂ cup dry white wine

2 Tbsp sour cream

Melt 1 Tbsp butter in a heavy skillet. Chop the sauerkraut finely. Put into the skillet and fry over low heat, stirring occasionally until the sauerkraut is dry, about 5-6 minutes. Remove it to a bowl. Put the remaining butter into the skillet and fry the onion until it begins to change color. Add the sauerkraut, sugar, salt if needed, pepper, and wine.

Cover tightly, and simmer on a very low heat for 45 minutes, stirring occasionally and making sure that there is enough liquid. Remove from the heat, and add the sour cream; stir until well blended. Cool completely before using.

Hot Sauerkraut Filling

In a large skillet, melt the butter and fry the onion, bacon, celery, and green pepper until they are limp. Add the sauerkraut, minced hot peppers, peppercorns, and season to taste. Fry slowly on low heat until the sauerkraut is cooked and the flavors well blended. Add an extra hot pepper if you want a tangier flavor. Remove the peppercorns and cool before using.

1-2 Tbsp butter

1 onion, chopped

1/2 cup diced bacon

1/2 cup chopped celery

1/2 cup chopped green pepper

3 cups drained sauerkraut

1-2 red or green hot peppers, minced

4-5 peppercorns

salt and pepper to taste

Sauerkraut and Mushroom Filling No. 1

Chop the sauerkraut very finely. In a large skillet, cook the onion in the fat until softened. Add the chopped mushrooms and stir fry for a couple of minutes. Add the sauerkraut, sour cream, salt and pepper. Cook over low heat until the sauerkraut is tender, and the flavors are blended. Do not overcook. Chill before using.

4 cups rinsed sauerkraut, well drained

1 onion, chopped

4 Tbsp bacon fat or butter

1 cup mushrooms, chopped

3 Tbsp sour cream

salt and pepper to taste

Sauerkraut and Mushrooms No. 2

1-2 Tbsp butter or margarine

¹/₂ cup diced bacon

1 onion, chopped

¹/₂ cup sliced mushrooms

1-2 tsp chopped fresh dill

3 cups rinsed, drained sauerkraut

3-4 Tbsp sweet cream

Melt the butter in a skillet. Fry the bacon for a couple of minutes, then add the onions, gently frying until they become soft. Add the mushrooms and dill. Fry for a couple of minutes to soften them; add the drained sauerkraut and the sweet cream. Stir occasionally. Continue cooking on low heat until the sauerkraut is cooked, and the mixture is very thick. Cool before using.

Sauerkraut with Dried Mushrooms Filling

¹/₂ cup dried mushrooms

1-2 cups warm water

salt to taste

3 onions, grated

3 Tbsp butter

1 Tbsp lemon juice

2 cups rinsed, drained sauerkraut, finely chopped

1-2 egg yolks, well-beaten (optional)

Soak the mushrooms in the water until tender. Cook in the soaking water, with a small amount of salt. Drain and chop the cooked mushrooms finely with a knife, or grind them. Sauté the onions in the butter in a skillet for 2-3 minutes. Add the mushrooms, the lemon juice, and the sauerkraut. Cook on medium-low heat, stirring occasionally, until the sauerkraut is limp. Cool before using, adding one or two beaten egg yolks to bind, if necessary.

Sauerkraut Filling
with Mushrooms and Beans

Pick over the beans and wash well. Soak overnight in a large saucepan. Drain and discard soaking water. Cover them with cold water, 3-4 times the depth of the beans. Bring to a boil, reduce heat, and simmer until well cooked. Drain. Rub the beans through a sieve, or mince them. Soak the mushrooms for at least 1 hour; then chop very finely or mince them. Chop the sauerkraut finely.

Fry the onions in oil in a skillet for about 2 minutes. Add the mushrooms, sauerkraut, and the seasonings, and continue to fry over low heat. When the sauerkraut and mushrooms are cooked, add the sieved beans and stir well to blend flavors. Adjust the seasonings. Cool well before using.

1 ½ cups kidney or pinto beans

¾ cup dried mushrooms

3 cups rinsed, well-drained sauerkraut

2 onions, grated

2 Tbsp oil

1-2 tsp salt, or to taste

pepper to taste

1 tsp paprika

As you may have noticed, cabbage and sauerkraut recipes are often interchangeable. If you do not like the tartness of sauerkraut nor the sweetness of cabbage, combine the two for a new flavor that is neither sweet nor sour, but has a hint of both.

Cabbage Filling No. 1

Finely slice one head of cabbage as for coleslaw. Sauté in butter, bacon fat, or lard until soft. Season with salt and pepper to taste. Cool.

1 head cabbage

3 Tbsp butter, bacon fat, or lard

salt and pepper to taste

Cabbage Filling No. 2

1 medium head of cabbage
boiling water

1 medium onion, chopped

4 Tbsp butter

1 Tbsp vinegar or lemon
juice

$1/2$ tsp sugar

salt and pepper to taste

Remove the outer leaves and the core from the cabbage. Cut the cabbage in coarse pieces and cook it, uncovered, in boiling water for about 6-8 minutes, but the cabbage should still be crisp. Drain, cool, and squeeze dry. Chop it very finely.

Fry the onion in butter in a skillet until translucent; add the cabbage, vinegar or lemon juice, sugar, and season to taste. Cook for a few minutes to blend the flavors. Chill uhoroughly.

Cabbage and Mushroom Filling

4 cups sauerkraut, squeezed
dry, or 2 lbs fresh cabbage

$1/2$ cup dried mushrooms

2 Tbsp butter

$1/2$ cup diced bacon

2 onions, chopped

6 peppercorns

2 Tbsp dried parsley

1 Tbsp chopped dill

salt and pepper to taste

If you are using cabbage, shred it finely, and squeeze as dry as you can.

Soak the mushrooms for 1-2 hours. Drain, reserving the liquid. Shred the mushrooms.

In a large skillet, melt the butter, and fry the bacon until it releases its fat. Add the onions, and continue frying until the onions are soft. Put the sauerkraut or cabbage into a saucepan to simmer with the liquid from the mushrooms. When partly cooked, add the bacon, onions, and mushrooms to the pot, with the peppercorns, parsley, and dill. Season to taste. When the sauerkraut or cabbage is cooked, the liquid should have been used up.

Cabbage and Ham Filling

Shred the cabbage finely. In a large skillet, melt the butter or bacon fat, and fry the onion gently until it has softened. Add the sauerkraut or the cabbage (or half of each), and fry until the cabbage is limp. Add the mushrooms, the ham, the lemon juice, dill, and the seasonings. Stir and continue frying gently until the cabbage is cooked. Use it well chilled.

1 medium head of cabbage, or 3 cups sauerkraut, squeezed dry, or half of each

4 tbsp butter or bacon fat

1 onion, diced

¹/₂ cup sliced mushrooms

1 cup finely chopped ham

1 Tbsp lemon juice

2 tsp chopped dill

salt and pepper to taste

Spicy Sausage Filling

Heat the oil in a large skillet. Add the onion and celery, and fry lightly. Add the cabbage or sauerkraut to the skillet. Continue cooking slowly until the cabbage is limp and beginning to brown. Add the basil, celery seed, garlic powder, the cayenne pepper, and the brown sugar. Season with salt and pepper. Add the finely chopped sausage. Cook a little longer to blend the flavors. Allow to cool before using.

1 Tbsp cooking oil

¹/₂ cup diced onion

¹/₂ cup chopped celery

2 cups finely chopped cabbage, or drained sauerkraut

1 ¹/₂ tsp dried basil

¹/₄ tsp celery seed

1 tsp garlic powder

¹/₈ tsp cayenne pepper

2-3 Tbsp brown sugar

salt and pepper to taste

1 ¹/₄ lb hot, spicy sausage, chopped finely

Sausage and Meat Filling

1 Tbsp cooking oil

1 onion, minced

2 cloves garlic, minced

1 lb lean ground beef

³/₄ lb ground sausage meat

2 cups parboiled rice

2 Tbsp tomato paste

1 Tbsp minced parsley

¹/₂ tsp mustard

salt and pepper to taste

Fillings for holubtsi or cabbage rolls, whether they are made with sauerkraut leaves or fresh cabbage, are numerous, many of them featuring meat mixed with the rice. Here is a traditional one featuring meat.

Heat the oil in a large non-stick skillet; add the onion and garlic, and fry gently until softened. Add the ground meats, and cook until they begin to lose color. Add the rice and the remaining ingredients. Continue cooking until the meat is cooked and the flavors well blended. Cool.

Sauerkraut Filling with Dried Fruit

1 cup dried pears

¹/₂ cup dried apricots

1 cup prunes

¹/₂ cup raisins

²/₃ cup sugar

2 cups rinsed, well-drained sauerkraut

¹/₂ cup water

1 Tbsp lemon juice

Chop the dried fruits very finely, or put through a grinder. Chop the sauerkraut very finely, or put through a grinder also.

Put the fruit and sauerkraut into a medium-sized saucepan with the water and lemon juice. Simmer slowly until the fruit is soft and the water is absorbed. Put the sugar in last, and stir until it is dissolved. You can vary the fruits to your taste.

Sauerkraut and Apricot Filling

In a medium-sized skillet, melt butter and fry onions until they are translucent. Add the sauerkraut, stir well, cooking until the sauerkraut is limp. Stir in the sugar, cinnamon stick, and the apricots. Cook a few minutes longer for the flavors to blend. Cool, and remove cinnamon stick before using.

2 Tbsp butter or margarine

1 cup diced onions

3 cups, rinsed, drained sauerkraut

2 tsp sugar

1 cinnamon stick

2 jars (7 1/2-oz each) strained apricots

Sauerkraut and Apple Filling

Chop the sauerkraut, the prunes, raisins, and apples very finely. Put into a medium-sized saucepan; adding the cinnamon stick and whole cloves tied in cheesecloth or in a tea ball, the water and lemon juice. Simmer slowly until the fruit is soft, and the water is absorbed. You may need a little more water if the fruit is very dry. Add enough brown sugar to taste. Discard the cinnamon stick and the cloves. Cool before using.

2 cups rinsed, squeezed dry, sauerkraut

1/2 cup prunes

1/2 cup raisins

1 3/4 cups chopped apples

1 cinnamon stick

3 whole cloves

1/2 cup water

1 Tbsp lemon juice

brown sugar to taste

Meat Dumplings for Soups

1 ¹/₂ lbs ground pork

1 ¹/₂ cups cooked rice

1 tsp salt

¹/₄ tsp pepper

2 eggs

2 tsp chopped dill

¹/₂ tsp savory

Mix all the ingredients thoroughly. Make into small balls, using wet hands. Drop them into boiling soup stock a few at a time.

Egg Drop Dumplings

3 to 4 eggs

¹/₂ to 1 cup of milk

¹/₂ to 1 tsp salt

3 to 4 cups all-purpose or unbleached flour

My family loves egg drop dumplings and I never seem to make enough for them. This recipe may be halved if you wish. The dough may be made quite thick, or fairly thin to drop into the soup in dribbles. I like mine thick enough to be dropped off a spoon. The dumpling may be varied by adding spices like paprika or such herbs as chopped dill or parsley to the dough.

Beat the eggs and milk; add the salt and flour together. Make a dough that is too soft to handle. Drop by half teaspoons (rough measure) into the boiling soup. Cover the pot with a tight lid and cook 3-5 minutes, watching closely, as dumplings can boil over very quickly.

Egg Drops

The previous egg drop dumplings recipe was used by my grandmother, my mother, and now by me, but cooks in other parts of Europe made these small dumplings in a slightly different way.

Beat the egg, and add the remaining ingredients, beating well until the batter is smooth. Pour the batter slowly from the end of a spoon in a thin stream into a simmering soup or milk, and let cook for 2-3 minutes. If poured from a height, the shape of the drops will be improved.

1 egg

4 Tbsp flour

1 Tbsp water

$^1/_8$ tsp salt

milk or soup

Spaetzle

German cooks long ago devised a method of making quick noodles. Spaetzle are used in soups or casseroles, browned in butter, enhanced with toasted bread crumbs, or Parmesan cheese, or served as a side dish to meat and game.

Sift flour and salt into a bowl. Make a depression in the centre and add the beaten eggs, mixing well. Slowly add the milk or water to make a smooth, thick dough. Press the dough through a colander or grater with large holes, or use a spaetzle maker. Drop the spaetzle into boiling, salted water. Do not crowd the spaetzle. Boil for 5-8 minutes or until cooked. Remove with a perforated spoon, rinse lightly with cold water and drain.

2 $^1/_4$ cups all-purpose or unbleached flour

1 tsp salt

3-4 eggs, well beaten

$^1/_4$ cup or more milk or water

Potato Dumplings

6 medium potatoes

2-3 eggs, beaten

1 cup or more all-purpose or unbleached flour

1 1/2 tsp salt

1 tsp dried dill or other herbs or spices

soup

Boil potatoes in their jackets. When cool enough to handle, peel; then mash thoroughly, leaving no lumps. Add eggs, flour, salt, and herbs or spices. Beat until the dough is light and smooth and thick enough to handle. Roll into small balls about 1 inch in diameter, and drop into boiling soup. Cook very quickly, 3-5 minutes until the puffed dumplings rise to the top of the soup.

Potato Dumpling No. 2

2 cups mashed potatoes

3/4 cup all-purpose or unbleached flour

1 egg, slightly beaten

1/2 cup dried bread crumbs

1/3 cup grated Cheddar cheese

salt and pepper

Here is another potato dumpling made with mashed potatoes and bread crumbs.

Mix all the ingredients together thoroughly. Season with salt and pepper to taste. The dough should be thick enough to roll. If not, add more flour. Place the dough on a floured board and roll to the thickness of a pencil. Cut into 1 1/2 to 2-inch lengths. Drop into boiling soup or boiling, salted water. Cook until they float to the top.

Liver Dumplings

This is a traditional German dumpling sometimes served over cooked sauerkraut or used as an accompaniment for meat dishes, especially pork ribs. You can use either beef, baby beef, or pork liver to make the dumplings.

Simmer liver in water for a few minutes. Remove all fibres. Put through a fine blade of the grinder.

Fry the onion in the fat together with the bread crumbs. Add to the ground liver with the beaten eggs, the lemon rind, the herbs, the salt and pepper. Stir in the flour, adding more if necessary to make the batter stiff enough to drop from a spoon.

Drop the batter into the boiling soup stock or broth a spoonful at a time. Cover the pot tightly and cook for 5-6 minutes, or until done. Serve with any sauerkraut dish.

1 ^{1}/$_2$ lbs liver

1 large onion, finely chopped

1 Tbsp butter or other cooking fat

3-4 cups bread crumbs

2 eggs, well beaten

1 tsp lemon rind

^{1}/$_4$ tsp marjoram

2 tsp dried parsley

1 ^{1}/$_2$ tsp salt

^{1}/$_2$ tsp pepper

^{1}/$_2$ cup flour

5-6 cups soup stock or broth

Liver Cakes

2 lbs liver

1 onion, grated

1 1/2 tsp salt

1/2 cup fine bread crumbs

2 Tbsp flour

1/2 tsp sage

1/4 tsp pepper

1 tsp grated lemon rind

1 egg

several slices bacon

For something different, try this version.

Simmer the liver in water for a few minutes. Grind or chop very finely. Mix all the ingredients together, except the bacon. Shape into round cakes and wrap each one in a slice of bacon. Secure with a toothpick if necessary. Fry in a hot skillet until well browned on both sides.

---

5 servings

Stuffed Apples

5 large baking apples

1 Tbsp margarine or butter

2 sticks celery, chopped

2 tsp chopped dill

2 tsp chopped parsley

1/2 tsp pepper

1/4 tsp caraway seeds (optional)

2 1/2 cups rinsed, drained sauerkraut, chopped

1/2 cup diced ham (optional)

1/4 cup dry white wine or water

These stuffed apples look good enough for dessert, but they are at their most delicious served with any pork dishes.

Prepare the apples by removing the stems and cutting off the top. Remove the cores. Scoop out the apples, leaving a 1/2-inch shell, and chop up the pulp. Preheat oven to 350° F.

Melt the margarine or butter in a large skillet. Add the celery, dill, parsley, the caraway if using, and the apple pulp. Add the sauerkraut and ham, frying slowly, stirring occasionally, until the sauerkraut starts changing color. Cool slightly, then fill the apple shells with it. Place the apples in a baking dish. Add the wine to the apples, and bake them until they are tender, basting frequently.

Dill Sauce

Dill sauce is frequently poured over cottage cheese buns, but it is equally good with a strudel, such as a Sauerkraut Strudel (see index), and is ideal over fresh, cooked vegetables, especially new potatoes.

In a medium-sized skillet, fry the onion and dill in butter. When they begin to turn color, add the cream, and simmer for 10-15 minutes. Serve with strudel or vegetables.

1 onion, chopped, or ³/₄ cup chopped green onions with tops

1-2 Tbsp chopped dill

2 Tbsp butter

2 cups whipping cream or half and half

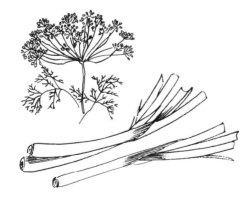

Herb Bouquets

Herb Bouquets

Herb bouquets or bouquet garni are made up of many herbs and spices. They are designed to enable you to use a number of different herbs in soups, stews, and meat gravies. Yet you have to be able to remove them quickly and efficiently. The herbs and spices are tied up in triple-layered cheesecloth squares measuring at least 6 inches by 6 inches or a small amount may be enclosed in a tea ball. Place in sealed jars to keep free of dust, and store in a cool, dark place to retain the color and avoid loss of flavor. They may be made up months ahead as long as they are kept dry and cool. Use as needed.

The kinds of herbs and spices to use are dictated by your recipe and your taste. There are as many combinations as are needed. My mother often used a spoonful or two of pickling spice which would have been impossible to remove had not the spices been enclosed in cheesecloth. Other bouquets may be made too. You may use any combination of many other herbs such as basil, celery, chervil, tarragon, burnet, rosemary, savory, dried red peppers, or chilies. Sometimes a powdered spice is added and, while it works its way out of the cheesecloth into the soup or stew, this is not of great importance.

It is difficult to give precise amounts for each bouquet. I change the amounts often, depending on what I am making and what flavors are to be combined. For instance, I like a spicy hot soup, and for that I may add extra cloves and a few peppercorns to a simple bouquet of pickling spice. Then, too, I'll add several hot, dried peppers, depending on the size of the pot, and how spicy I want the food. The combinations are endless, all depending on your taste buds. Beginning cooks should use the herbs and spices in the amounts suggested, but as you begin to recognize what you like, do not hesitate to change both.

Herb Bouquets

(continued)

Bouquets of dried herbs are better and more effective if you try to include at least one fresh herb such as celery leaves, parsley, dill, or any others. For the best result, do not leave the herbs in the soup any longer than 1 hour. Each bouquet sachet is designed to flavor 2-3 quarts of soup.

Here are some popular combinations, numbered for easier choice.

Herb Bouquet No. 1

1 sachet

Mix all ingredients together well. Tie securely into a square of cheesecloth.

1 bay leaf

3-4 sprigs parsley

several sprigs of dill, or 1-2 tsp dillweed

3-5 whole cloves

$^1/_2$ tsp or less thyme as it is strong flavored

Herb Bouquet No. 2

1 sachet

Mix all ingredients together well. Tie securely into a square of cheesecloth.

4 sprigs of parsley

3 cloves of garlic

1 bay leaf

4 sprigs of dill

$^3/_4$ tsp thyme

3-4 whole cloves

Herb Bouquet No. 3

6 bay leaves

6 whole cloves

1 cup celery flakes

1 tsp marjoram

¹/₄ cup parsley flakes

³/₄ tsp peppercorns

¹/₂ tsp ground savory

2 tsp ground thyme

Each sachet will flavor 2 quarts of liquid.

Put 1 bay leaf and 1 whole clove in each of 6 cheesecloth squares. Mix the remaining ingredients together and divide into 6 equal parts, adding one part to each square. Tie each sachet securely.

24 sachets for soups

Herb Bouquet No. 4

¹/₄ cup thyme

¹/₄ cup marjoram

¹/₄ cup parsley flakes

¹/₂ cup celery flakes

2 Tbsp ground savory

1 tsp ground sage

1 Tbsp crumbled bay leaves

Mix all ingredients together well. Divide into 24 portions and tie each into a square of cheesecloth.

Herb Bouquet No. 5

2 sachets

Mix all ingredients together well. Tie securely into a square of cheesecloth.

4-6 sprigs parsley

¹/₂ tsp thyme

1 tsp chervil

6 sprigs dill

4 bay leaves

4-6 whole cloves

2-3 cloves garlic

8-10 peppercorns

Herb Bouquet No. 6

1 sachet

Here's a very simple one.

Mix all ingredients together well. Tie securely into a square of cheesecloth.

1 Tbsp whole mixed pickling spices

some fresh parsley, celery leaves, or both

Further Reading

Blinn, Johna. *Fabulous Soups*, N.Y.: Playmore Inc., 1983.

Brizova, Joza. *The Czechoslovak Cookbook*, N.Y.: Crown Publishers Inc., 1965.

Casella, Dolores. *A World of Baking*, N.Y.: David White, Inc. 1968.

Cleveland "R" Club. *Just a Pinch of Russian*, Cleveland: Federated Russian Orthodox Clubs, 1972.

Creasy, Rosalind. *Cooking From the Garden*, San Francisco: Sierra Book Clubs, 1972.

Family Circle Illustrated Library of Cooking, Rockville Centre, New York: Rockville House Pub. Inc., 1972.

Favorite Recipes of America: Meats, Louisville, Kentucky: Favorite Recipes Press, 1968.

Georgievsky, Melman, Shadura, Shemjakinsky. *Ukrainian Cuisine*, USSR: Georgievsky & Co., 1975.

Gotlieb, Sondra. *Cross Canada Cooking*, Vancouver: Hancock House Publishing Ltd., 1976.

Green, Karen. *The Great International Noodle Experience*, Toronto: McClellan and Stewart, Ltd., 1977.

Jost Voth, Norma. *Mennonite Foods and Folkways From South Russia*, Vol. I, Intercourse, PA: Goodbooks, 1990.

Kramarz, Inge. *The Balcan Cookbook*, N.Y.: Crown Publishing Inc., 1972.

Lyons Bar-David, Molly. *The Israeli Cookbook*, N.Y. Crown Publishing, Inc., 1964.

Montagne, Prosper. *Larouse Gastronomic*, N.Y.: Crown Publishing Inc., 1977.

Ochorowicz-Monatowa, Maya. *Polish Cookery*, N.Y.: Crown Publishing Inc., 1974.

Pisetska Farley, Marta. *Festive Ukrainian Cooking*, Pittsburgh, PA: University of Pittsburgh Press, 1990.

Rombauer, Irma S. and Marion R Becker. *The Joy of Cooking*, Indiananpolis: Bobbs-Merrill Company Inc., 1931.

Schuler, Elizabeth. *German Cookery*, N.Y.: Crown Publishing Inc., 1955.

Shaw Nelson, Kay. *Complete International Salad Book*, N.Y.: Stern/Day Publishers, 1978.

Sheraton, Mimi. *The German Cookbook*, N.Y.: Random House Inc., 1965.

Staebler, Edna. *Food That Really Schmecks – Mennonite Country Cooking*, Toronto: McGraw-Hill Ryerson Ltd., 1968.

Stechishin, Savella. *Traditional Ukrainian Cookery*, Winnipeg: Trident Press Ltd., 1973.

Teubner, Christian, and Annette Waltner. *The Best of Salads and Buffets*, Tucson, Arizona: H.P. Books, 1990.

Ukrainian Women's Association of Canada. *Ukrainian Daughter's Cookbook*, Regina: Ukrainian Women's Association of Canada, 1984.

Ying, Mildred, ed. *The New Good Housekeeping Cookbook*, N.Y.: Hearst Publishing, 1986.

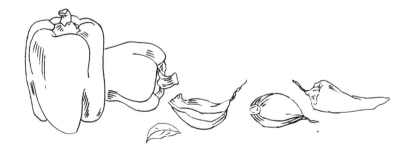

Index